The
Mastiff

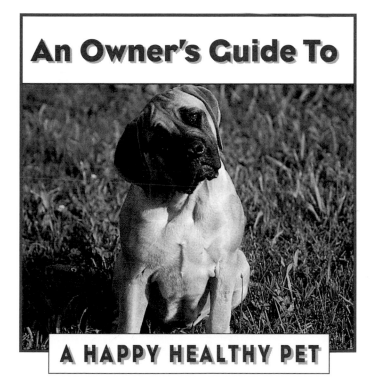

An Owner's Guide To

A HAPPY HEALTHY PET

Howell Book House

Howell Book House

A Simon & Schuster Macmillan Company
1633 Broadway
New York, NY 10019

Macmillan Publishing books may be purchased for business or sales promotional use.
For information please write: Special Markets Department, Macmillan Publishing
USA, 1633 Broadway, New York, NY 10019.

Library of Congress Cataloging-in-Publication Data
Becknell, John.
The mastiff: an owner's guide to a happy, healthy pet / John Becknell.
p. cm.
ISBN 0-87605-609-5
1. Mastiffs. I. Title. II. Series.
SF429.M36M36 1998
636.73–dc21   98-14483
                   CIP

Manufactured in the United States of America
10 9 8 7 6 5 4 3 2 1

Series Director: Amanda Pisani
Series Assistant Director: Rich Thomas
Book Design by Michele Laseau
Cover Design by Iris Jeromnimon
Illustration: Steve Adams
Photography:
  Front cover by Mary Bloom
  Back cover by Paulette Braun (Pets by Paulette)
  Paulette Braun (Pets by Paulette): 13, 21, 31, 41, 58, 62, 65, 67
  Howell Book House: 14, 19, 23
  Bob Schwartz: i, 2–3, 5,7, 8, 9, 16, 22, 24, 29, 33, 36–37, 38, 39, 48, 49, 52, 60, 63, 68,
    69, 72, 76, 79, 91
  Theresa Terry: 11, 25, 27, 46, 50
Production Team: Toi Davis, Clint Lahnen, Angel Perez, Heather Pope,
  Dennis Sheehan, Terri Sheehan

Contents

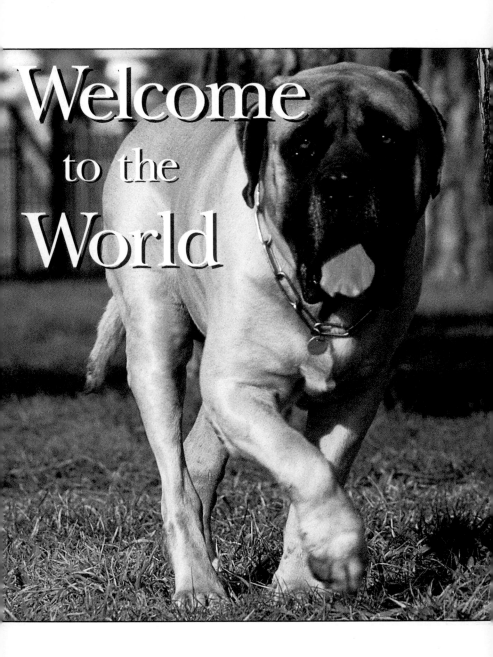

Welcome
to the
World

of the
Mastiff

External Features of the Mastiff

Occiput

Stop

Muzzle

Flews

Shoulder

Chest

Pastern

Withers

Back

Loin

Croup

Stifle

Dewclaw

Hock

chapter 1

What Is a Mastiff?

Welcome to the big world of Mastiffs. The gentle giant you have chosen to learn about is an ancient and fascinating breed as noble and grand today as it was when it stood fiercely on battlefields and graced the courts of kings. The Mastiff has a long history as a guard dog, war dog, fighting dog and hunter, and has survived near extinction twice in this century to emerge as a faithful and loyal pet.

Initially, people are always most impressed with the sheer size of the Mastiff. Standing more than 3 feet tall and often weighing more than his owner, this dog will fill the back seat of a car and take up most of a couch (if you let him). Yet, the Mastiff carries his size with a quiet, solid, majestic dignity that suggests the large amount of devotion this pet will return to those who spend time with him. Endearing, with a dark face and a puzzled, mournful expression that seems to hold the secrets of some sad event from long ago, the Mastiff we know today has developed into a wonderful companion dog that is now known more for his quiet, comforting presence than his fierce presentation. Faithful, almost to a fault, the Mastiff's devotion will amaze you, and the following chapters will help you understand him, how to care for him and how you can create a healthy and fulfilling relationship with this magnificent animal.

The Breed Standard

Around the world there are a number of similar large dogs known as Mastiffs. Some are more alike than others, but the purebred dog that this book addresses is a breed that in the recent past was called the Old English Mastiff, or OEM. The purebred Mastiff as we know it today has been bred to a "standard," or particular description that has been agreed upon and approved by breeders to represent the ideal or perfection for that breed. Breeders strive to match and produce animals that will come as close to the standard as possible. The ideal is always being pursued and has yet to be achieved. The standard is also used as a guide for judging the animal in dog shows. Any deviation from the standard is called a "fault." The American version of the standard was written and approved by the American Kennel Club and the Mastiff Club of America and was last revised and approved in 1991.

When considering whether or not a Mastiff is right for you, the standard is a good starting point for the prospective owner to appreciate the unique aspects of the Mastiff and which characteristics are desired. The rest of this chapter will review the standard in layman's terms. If you are unfamiliar with the various parts of a dog, use the "External Features of the Mastiff" chart on page 4, which shows the common terminology breeders use. Direct quotes from the standard will appear in italics with comments appearing in regular type. For a complete copy of the Mastiff AKC Standard you can write to the American Kennel Club, 5580 Centerview Dr., Raleigh, NC 27690-0643, or download it from the AKC Web site at http://www.akc.org/mastif.htm.

APPEARANCE AND SIZE

The Mastiff is a large, powerful and solid-looking dog. He has a broad, dark head; drooping ears; a broad, short muzzle and a short, coarse fawn-, brindle- or apricot-colored coat. The Mastiff should strike the observer with an impression, not just of size, but one of *grandeur and dignity*. This look should come from the dog appearing *symmetrical* and having a *well-knit frame,* which means the dog's size and weight should be balanced with an appropriate bone structure to support it.

Most females are smaller than males and this is not faulted, providing the female portrays the same solid *proportionally powerful structure* seen in the male.

The Mastiff is an exceptionally large dog!

THE HEAD

Apart from size, the head is one of the most fascinating aspects of the Mastiff. From its huge size to its powerful jaws and wrinkled expressions, the head gives this big animal his beauty. To those unfamiliar with Mastiffs, the dog's head may appear heavy and unnecessarily wide, but it fits the body and was purposely developed this way to give the dog a powerful grip with his jaws and yet still allow him to breathe freely. The description of the head is the largest section in the standard and for a good reason—it is best seen and difficult to describe. In general, the head should have *a massive appearance when viewed from any angle* with *breadth greatly desired.*

Newcomers to this breed are often surprised by this dog's compelling expression. A Mastiff can melt your heart or scare the devil out of a stranger with his expression. Ideally, breeders strive for a dog that appears kind and alert but not predatory. Of course the soul of a dog's expression is in his **eyes** and the Mastiff's eyes should fit the general contours of the face, *be medium in size, set wide apart* and as dark brown as possible without showing any haw (the red membranous edges surrounding the eye). The downward hanging V-shaped **ears** should be set wide apart at the highest point of the skull, and when relaxed should rest close against the cheeks. The color of the ears should match the color of the muzzle—*the blacker the better.*

Broad, deep, full and strong are all characteristics of a proper Mastiff muzzle.

The Mastiff's **skull** should not be domed but *appear broad and somewhat flattened between the ears.* The line across the ears and skull should be continuous. The space between the eyes—the **stop**—should be notice-

able and form a distinct angle change between the forehead and muzzle but not be too abrupt. The ridges just above the eyes should be *moderately raised.*

One of the most engaging characteristics of the Mastiff is the skin wrinkles on the forehead that give him his sad or quizzical look. According to the standard, these wrinkles should be seen when the dog is relaxed and become *particularly distinctive when at attention.* But the dog should not be over-wrinkled with excessive folds of flesh rolling down the sides of the cheeks. When no wrinkles are seen the head is described as being "dry."

The Mastiff's powerful **muzzle** needs to be broad and deep and appear full and strong. The muzzle is evaluated in both length and circumference as compared to the overall size of the head. The proper length of the muzzle should be one third the length of the entire head (as measured from the back of the skull, the occiput, to the tip of the nose). The circumference of the muzzle (measured midway between the eyes and the tip of the nose) should be three-fifths of the circumference of the head measured just in front of the ears. When the muzzle is too long, it is referred to as being snippy. From the eyes to the end of the nose, the muzzle should maintain its width and have a full broad under-jaw. Both the muzzle and **nose** need to be black, and again the standard suggests *the blacker the better.* The nostrils should be flat against the nose and *not pointed or turned up.*

The powerful **jaws** of the Mastiff are covered with large full lips that hang down at such an angle as to give a *modified square profile.* The teeth should ideally meet each other evenly in what is called a scissors or level bite. Some Mastiffs will have an undershot jaw like a Boxer in which the lower jaw protrudes beyond the upper jaw. This is acceptable providing it is not pronounced and the teeth are not seen when the mouth is closed.

THE BODY

With a long history that includes being a war dog and hunter, the size of the Mastiff has always been one of his greatest attributes. The Mastiff's loyal and usually laid-back disposition seems all the more significant when matched with his size. It's difficult to feel alone or ignored when a dog as large as a Mastiff comes between you and the television for a little attention. Adult males usually weigh between 160 and 230 pounds, and females around 120 to 170 pounds. If you are new to Mastiffs it's important to be around a full-grown male to appreciate how large a Mastiff can become. Males over 200 pounds are common. Occasionally a female

It is not uncommon for a Mastiff to weigh more than 200 pounds!

will become this large. The standard sets no upper limit on how large a Mastiff can be; according to the *Guinness Book of World Records,* the world's largest dog was a Mastiff weighing 343 pounds.

However much a Mastiff weighs, the standard expects the dog to symmetrically fit his body and stipulates minimum heights. Males must be at least 30 inches to the shoulder and females must be 27½ inches, but it's important that a Mastiff not appear too tall or gangly. Height should come from depth of body rather than the leg, and in the approximate proportions of two-thirds body to one-third leg. The powerful massive appearance will come from the rectangular shape of the dog's well-developed muscles and heavy bones. The body should be somewhat longer than it is high.

The powerful look of the Mastiff continues into the **neck,** which may appear short because of the large size of the head and body, but it is described as being of *medium length and slightly arched.* As the neck descends from the head, it will gradually get larger as it approaches the shoulder and should not be wrinkled.

Important to the appearance of carrying his weight solidly is how the top of the back appears in profile. Breeders call this the **topline** and ideally there should be no dips or humps nor should it drop off sharply behind the rump. The ideal topline should be *straight, level, and firm.* Like the rest of the body, the back should appear *muscular, powerful, and straight* and as you look at the Mastiff from the rear, you should see a slight rounding over the rump or croup as it descends to the tail, but it should not slope or fall away. The thighs should appear *wide and muscular.*

Creating an image of unmovable power similar to that of a football lineman, the **chest** of the ideal Mastiff is wide, deep, rounded and will come down to the level of the elbows in the mature dog. The forechest or the very front part of the chest should be *deep and well defined with the breast bone extending in front of the foremost point of the shoulders.*

The **tail** is wide at its roots, set on *moderately high* and then tapers down hanging to the hocks or a little longer. If the tail is set on too low, it gives the hindquarters an unacceptable downward slope. When the dog is standing relaxed, the tail should hang straight and when on the move or excited a slight curve upward is expected, but it should never be up over the back.

THE FOREQUARTERS

The forequarters include the shoulders, legs, pasterns (the part of the leg just above the foot) and the feet. The shoulders should appear powerful and firm, sloping moderately with the front angulation matching that of the rear angulation. Again, the front legs should appear strong with solid bones and be set widely apart. As the legs descend, the elbows should be parallel to the body and should not stick out. The pasterns, the shock absorbers for the Mastiff, should appear strong and only slightly bent. Consistent with the rest of the forequarters, the feet should be large, as they bear a tremendous amount of weight. They should be round, almost catlike, with the toes arched, and they should turn neither out nor in. According to the standard, black toenails are preferred.

A Mastiff's feet should be large, as they carry a great deal of weight.

THE HINDQUARTERS

The hindquarters include the hips, the thighs, the stifle joint, the lower legs and the rear feet. When looking at the dog from the rear, the hindquarters should appear squarely set, *broad, wide, and muscular* and be in balance with the angulation of the front shoulders. The rear legs should be wide apart, again parallel, giving the Mastiff the appearance of solid grounding. From the side, the thighs should appear *well developed leading to a strong hock joint.* The stifle joint or the "knee" should match the angle of the front.

The standard goes into some detail about the angles of stifle joints. A straight stifle joint (a straight line running from hock to hip) is not permitted. The standard explains the proper angle in detail: *When the portion of the leg below the hock is correctly "set back" and stands perpendicular to the ground, a plumb line dropped from the rearmost point of the hind quarter will pass in front of the foot. This rules out straight hocks, and since stiffle angulation varies with hock angulation, it rules out insufficiently angulated stifles.*

COAT AND COLOR

The coat and colors of the Mastiff contribute greatly to his majestic appearance. There can be some variation in the coat length of the Mastiff, with some being long-coated like a St. Bernard and some with a short Doberman-type coat, but neither type is ideal. According to the standard, the coat should be *moderately short*, straight and coarse. The dense, short undercoat should lie close to the body. The standard warns against a coat that is long enough to produce a *fringe* on the belly, tail or hind legs.

Officially, only three colors are allowed for the Mastiff. These colors are fawn, brindle and apricot. Of course, the muzzle, ears, nose and areas around the eyes extending upward must always be dark and, as always, *the blacker the better*. The body colors can vary. Fawn is a color between tan and light brown and can vary from very light to a color almost bordering on the red of apricot or dark brown. Brindle describes clearly defined black stripes on a fawn or apricot background and the standard suggests that the *background color should be completely covered with very dark stripes.* Apricot is a reddish-orange color that makes a compelling contrast to the black muzzle and ears. A small patch of white on the chest is permitted (and often seen on the toes), but excessive white on the chest or any other part of the body is faulted in showing, as is a lack of dark color on the mask, ears or nose.

GAIT

As expected, the way a Mastiff moves needs to be in keeping with his grand size and dignified presentation. When watching a Mastiff move toward you, you should see an animal that moves freely with the suggestion of power and strength. As he passes by, you will not see the grace of a Great Dane but more the strength and power of a draft horse with the rear legs providing the drive and the front legs tracking smoothly with a good forward reach. The legs should move *straight forward and as the dog's speed increases from a walk to a trot, the feet should move in toward the center line of the body to maintain balance.*

TEMPERAMENT

No matter how big or small a dog is, when choosing a pet, companion or helper, temperament is one of the most important parts of the animal's makeup. While Mastiffs have an ancient history as fierce guard and soldier dogs, today they are considered to be a sensitive, gentle, quiet breed that is laid-back and eager to please. According to the standard, an ideal Mastiff should portray a combination *of grandeur, good nature, courage, and docility* with dignity being preferred

Mastiffs are generally calm, gentle and quiet animals.

over gaiety. Such a description covers a lot of territory, and it may be difficult to see all these characteristics in the same dog. But in general terms, with proper socialization the Mastiff has the sort of temperament that lends itself to being a great companion and pet. Most Mastiff owners will describe their dogs as great gentle beasts that are fiercely loyal, willing to protect their people and property, but on most days are quite content to find a soft place on a rug and take a good nap.

Not a Breed for Everyone

This is the official Mastiff. It's not for everyone, but if you're attracted to this breed and willing to invest the time, many rewards await you. The following chapters will tell you more about Mastiffs and prepare you for one of your own.

chapter 2

The Mastiff's Ancestry

Breeding a dog to a specific written standard is a modern idea. Only in the last 150 years have people begun to strictly separate various types of dogs, keep breeding lines pure and document their pedigrees. Therefore, the history of a purebred dog is fairly modern. However, a few types of dogs can be traced back to long before the times of recorded pedigrees.

History

The Mastiff is one of the types of dogs that predate recorded pedigrees. It belongs to a whole group of large fighting and guard dogs with an ancient history. This history is found in numerous artifacts from the Middle East, Asia and Europe and appears in countless writings, including the work of Herodotus, Caesar, Marco Polo, Chaucer and Shakespeare.

Ancient Warrior

While the Mastiff-type dog may be as old as man's relation with canines, the first known glimpse comes from a 5000-year-old artifact taken from the Babylonian palace of Ashurbanipal. The artifact, now on display at the British Museum in London, depicts large Mastiff-type dogs hunting lions in the desert near the Tigris River. While thinner and perhaps taller than the Mastiff we know today, there is no mistaking the head and general shape as being Mastiff. Mastiff-type dogs appear in numerous ancient Asian art works and appear in Chinese literature around 1121 B.C.

Much of what we know about the ancient Mastiff comes from tales about its legendary fierceness and prowess in fighting and warring. According to one tale told by Herodotus, Cyrus the Great (founder of the Persian Empire) was given a Mastiff as a gift by the King of Albania in about 550 B.C. In those days, the value of a good dog was determined by how well it fought against other dogs and wild beasts. Needing to test the gift, Cyrus matched the Mastiff against one of his Persian dogs, and then against a bull. But the dog would not fight. It was shy and turned away from its opponents. So with typical royal contempt for the gift, Cyrus had the cowardly Mastiff killed. Eventually word of the dog's performance and death traveled back to the King of Albania. Whether he was angry or embarrassed is not known, but he sent Cyrus another dog, a ferocious Mastiff bitch. Along with the dog he sent the message that this Mastiff was no ordinary dog, and she would think nothing of ripping apart a Persian dog or a bull. In fact, he taunted Cyrus, this dog needed to be put up against a really worthy opponent like a lion or even an elephant. Then he warned Cyrus that Mastiffs were a rare and royal gift and he would not send another. Cyrus, perhaps amused at the King of Albania's boast, immediately set the dog against a huge elephant. As Herodotus tells the tale, the Mastiff attacked with such vicious fury and determination that the elephant was driven to its knees and would have been killed by the Mastiff had she not been pulled away.

Whether or not this story is true will never be known, but it does suggest the legendary reputation that the Mastiff has maintained throughout history. Caesar describes the Mastiff in his accounts of the Roman invasion of England in 55 B.C., and it is reported that Hannibal, another great Roman leader, took several battalions of trained war Mastiffs as he crossed the Alps in his sweep of Europe. In writing about his travels in Asia, Marco Polo tells of 5,000 Mastiffs being kept in a kennel by Kubla Khan to be used for hunting and war, and it is also recorded that Henry VIII of England gave Charles V of France some 400 Mastiffs to be used as fighting dogs in battle.

Ornaments and keepsakes such as the one pictured here provide a vehicle for passing on a love for the breed from generation to generation.

We're not exactly sure how Mastiffs were used on the battlefield, but it can be surmised that they were used as pulling dogs, as guards and as forward weapons to confront and attack the enemy. This seems consistent with the Mastiff's reputation as an attacking fighter. Roman records tell of Mastiffs being exported from England specifically for use in bloody competitions, like those in the Coliseum. The dogs were pitted against numerous opponents including bears, lions, tigers, bulls, other dogs and even human gladiators.

Evidence of the Mastiff's ancient past and widespread use exist outside the historical accounts as well. Undoubtedly, everywhere the Mastiff went, it bred with local dogs, and breed experts believe that many of the large dogs around the world can trace their origins to the Mastiff. They feel quite certain that Mastiff blood is in numerous modern breeds, such as the St. Bernard (where the connection is obvious), as well as very different breeds such as the Chow Chow and Pug.

THE MASTIFF IN ENGLAND

While evidence of the Mastiff is scattered around the world, the dog as we know it today certainly had its roots on the British Isles. How the breed came to England is unknown. Some theorize that it was imported by ancient Phoenician sailors while others suggest the Mastiff was indigenous to the British Isles and developed by the ancient and mysterious Celtic warriors it accompanied to battle. Perhaps it's enough to know that when the Romans invaded, nearly 2,000 years ago, the Mastiff was already a firm fixture on the British landscape.

The role of the Mastiff in England during the feudal Middle Ages was primarily that of guard dog. The land was untamed and rife with bandits, wolves and other wild animals that posed a constant threat to the peasant farmers and feudal manors. During daylight hours people were relatively safe and the Mastiffs were kept tied up, and thus became known as *tiedogs* or *bandogs*. But when darkness came and lurking dangers became a real threat, Mastiffs were released to roam around the village and countryside in order to chase away unwanted visitors and warn the people of impending attack. Laws of the time decreed that villages were required to keep at least two tiedogs.

Apparently these night-roving Mastiffs were not just chasing wild dangers, but getting into trouble as roaming dogs are prone to do. In the Forest Laws of 1017, we find it is specifically decreed that Mastiffs (along with several other breeds) have three toes from one front foot cut off to prevent them from chasing the king's deer. (The Mastiff was not a fast runner, but it was apparently being blamed for developing a taste for venison.)

As the Mastiff became recognized for its guarding capabilities, it was also recognized as a faithful and loyal companion. During the raucous Hundred Years War between England and France, a Sir Piers Legh of Lyme Hall took a bitch Mastiff with him to the War in France. During the battle of Agincourt in 1415, Piers was severely wounded and left helpless on the battlefield. The Mastiff faithfully stayed by his side, comforting him and protecting him from plunderers. When the battle ended, Piers was found by English soldiers and carried to Paris with the courageous and loyal Mastiff still by his side. Eventually Piers succumbed to his wounds and the dog was sent back to Lyme Hall where she became the ancestor of the now famous Lyme Hall Mastiffs—a line that endured until the beginning of this century. Today, in a drawing room at Lyme Hall, a picture of the brave Mastiff with her gallant master has been preserved in an old stained-glass window.

While the Lyme Hall Mastiffs had narrow heads and tapered muzzles, it is obvious from drawings of the time that this ancestor was very similar to the modern Mastiff. The Lyme Hall kennel keepers insisted on keeping the line pure and would only allow the dogs to be bred at Lyme Hall. It is during this time that the Mastiff begins to shed its image as only a fighter and guard dog and appears more frequently in historical accounts and pictures as a companion and pet.

Unfortunately, a more expansive view of the Mastiff did not save it from the popular bloody sport of bull- and bearbaiting during the reign of Elizabeth I. While the sport spawned great interest in the Mastiff and its numbers grew, the interest was mainly in its size and fighting abilities. Mastiffs were trained to attack, and once placed in a ring were expected to kill or be killed in a confrontation with other dogs (or other animals such as bulls, bears and boars). These bloody duels were staged for the amusement of the nobility, clergy and peasantry and led to a violent death for many Mastiffs. Even though the sport was outlawed in 1835, it continued underground for some years and still goes on in some parts of the world today. Fortunately, the Mastiff is no longer considered to be a prize fighting dog.

The Mastiff in the Nineteenth and Twentieth Centuries

As the interest in bullbaiting died out and the need for large guard dogs waned, so did the Mastiff's numbers. But early in the nineteenth century, the Mastiff became the prize of a few nobles and admiring breeders, including Mr. T.H. Lukey (called the father of the modern Mastiff), who were interested in preserving the animal and began to carefully breed the Mastiff. During this time there was a significant amount of crossbreeding between Alpines (St. Bernards) and Regency Bulldogs as breeding stock was limited and some breeders felt the need to improve the breed. This crossbreeding caused a fair amount of vehement discussion, preserved for us in their correspondence, between the breeders.

As the breed moved into the nineteenth and twentieth centuries, it faced many challenges.

The last half of the nineteenth century was a golden period for dogs in England. Interest in all breeds led to the organization of formal dog shows, and in 1873 the English Kennel Club was formed to encourage registration, maintain official pedigree records and clarify breed standards. This was also a golden period for the

Mastiff in particular. In 1883, the Old English Mastiff Club was formed, and there was a significant increase in interest and numbers. Pictures from the early days of the club portray a large dog we easily recognize as today's Mastiff.

As expected, the early days of the Old English Mastiff Club were marked by extensive and passionate debating, arguing and even bickering about what constituted a true Mastiff. Again, from correspondence between breeders and, at this point, in newspaper articles, we can see that few agreed on which characteristics were ideal. Most of the arguments were about head shape, muzzles and whether or not crossbreeding or tainted dogs should be allowed.

But even the formations of a club and formalized dog shows were not enough to keep the breed strong. The Mastiff's numbers seemed unavoidably destined to wax and wane. By 1900 the numbers had diminished again, with only a few dogs being registered. Once again this shortage of breeding stock led to more crossbreeding, mainly with the Bulldog, which again became a hot bone of contention among breeders. Those who crossbred insisted that they were improving the breed, while the purists argued that an ideal dog had already been achieved. Certainly the crossbreeding with the Bulldog led to a broader muzzle but eventually, as crossbreeds were assimilated, the discussion died out and the Bull Mastiff emerged as a breed of its own.

FAMOUS MASTIFF OWNERS

Kubla Khan

Hannibal—the Roman military leader

King Henry VIII

George C. Scott

Marlon Brando

Kirsty Alley

Bob Dylan

FLEA—bass guitarist for Red Hot Chilli Peppers

Randy Bish—political cartoonist

A Breed in Peril

The ancient Mastiff thrived on war, but the two major wars of the twentieth century were extremely hard on the breed. During World War I, the Mastiff's numbers, like those of the young English soldiers who fought on the continent, were decimated. The war brought incredible shortages and a very somber mood to England. Resources became scarce and, not surprisingly,

keeping a big dog that could eat as much as a soldier was considered to be counter to the war effort. It's difficult to imagine now, but entire kennels of dogs were destroyed and the Mastiff's future in England was placed in serious peril. Ironically, a few Mastiffs, true to their ancient calling, found their way to the war and can be seen in pictures pulling gun carriages and ammunition carts.

Following World War I, the Mastiff's numbers slowly began to grow, but not without the help of some dedicated

breeders and kennel keepers. The three most significant kennels of that time were Mr. & Mrs. Scheerboom's Havengore Mastiffs, Miss Bell's Withybush Line and Mr. & Mrs. Oliver's Hellingly Kennels. The devotion and care of these breeders had a tremendous influence on the Mastiff and once again reestablished the breed.

During the world wars, the English population found that keeping a dog was a luxury that it painfully had to do without.

But again, this growth was only temporary. In the late 1930s the registered breeding stock was decreased when the Olivers' kennel closed and a number of its prize dogs were sent to America. And then war struck again. This time, as German planes began to pound Britain, nothing but survival was in the British mind. As before there were no resources for dogs—especially large ones. Breeding stopped and again many dogs were destroyed or sent to America. It is during this time that the breed nearly became extinct in England. By the end of the war, there was little or no breeding stock left and the Mastiff, as an English breed, appeared doomed.

But the British are dog lovers to the core and even though they were forced to import breeding stock of a dog that had once been native to their land, they returned the Mastiff to its ancient home and once again its numbers grew.

Through the 1950s the breed was firmly reestablished and has continued to grow through the efforts of devoted English Mastiff lovers and breeders. Today in England a few old manor kennels keep dozens of Mastiffs as in the days of old, but most Mastiffs are kept singly or in pairs as house pets.

THE MASTIFF IN AMERICA

Although it's difficult to substantiate, the Mastiff may have come to America with the Pilgrims on the Mayflower as one of two dogs—a Spaniel or a Mastiff. Beginning in the colonial period, large Mastiff-type dogs appeared frequently in art and literature. As in England, the dog was primarily used as a guard dog on plantations and farms—though there is some evidence that it was used in bull-baiting types of competitions. Undoubtedly the dog was mixed with numerous other breeds and the purebred American Mastiff we know today came later from English breeding lines.

The Mastiff Club of America was formed in 1929.

As interest in dog breeding and showing grew on both sides of the Atlantic in the mid-to-late-nineteenth century, a number of Mastiffs began to appear in America. There were few restrictions and no quarantine for dogs imported from England, and by the end of the century there was a number of Mastiffs registered with the American Kennel Club.

And then, mimicking the same roller coaster history as in England, the numbers began to decline until 1912 when there were no registered Mastiffs. The breed may have completely disappeared in the United States had it not been reintroduced by breeders in Canada after World War I.

The Mastiff in England and America owes much to C.W. Dickinson of Toronto, Canada. Dickinson founded the now famous Canadian Wingfield Kennels with dogs imported from England. Dickinson's contribution was not only in breeding a fine line of Mastiffs, but in keeping the Mastiff alive when its numbers were dangerously low. The pedigree books from the Wingfield Kennels show that the shortage of breeding stock was often critical and led to in-breeding

The Mastiff continues to be a successful breed, in both America and the U.K.

and even a full brother-sister mating. With today's concerns about genetic strength and testing, such practices would be avoided, but they do remind us of the Mastiff's precarious existence and the dedication breeders have had to this dog. Almost all Mastiffs today have in one way or another descended from Wingfield breeding.

By 1929, the breed was firmly established and the Mastiff Club of America was formed with the objective of preserving and protecting the breed. The breed continues to become more and more popular in America, and through the last several decades the breed's numbers have soared. Today, America has more Mastiffs than anywhere else in the world. There are numerous breeders spread throughout the continent with a number of very active and energetic regional clubs working diligently to preserve and protect this magnificent animal.

chapter 3

The World According to the Mastiff

Do you truly wish to share a portion of your life with a Mastiff? The Mastiff is a very large dog, with an awesome (some would say fierce) appearance and a long tradition of protecting its owners and standing solidly in the midst of trouble, but other than as a passing curiosity, why would anyone want one today?

As its history as a working dog demonstrates, the Mastiff has played a number of roles as a fighter, a guard, a pulling and hauling dog and even as a search and rescue dog. The Mastiff can still do all of these jobs but, arguably, there are other breeds that are now better suited for these tasks. Besides, most of us aren't looking for a working dog.

The reason to have a Mastiff should come from a powerful attraction to and appreciation for very large dogs, and an intense desire to develop a close relationship with an animal that will become a significant part of your life as a pet, a companion and a dependent. The decision to own (or as some would say, be owned by) a Mastiff is a decision you should make only after much thought, consideration and consultation with everyone in your household. As most owners will tell you, a Mastiff can be a big, big pile of trouble and a lot of work. But they will also tell you that beneath the huge exterior of this animal you will find an extremely loyal friend that craves your attention and affirmation, is an excellent companion and whose gift to you is an endless stream of comfort, amusement and joy.

The World of Big Dogs

First, ask what it is you want from a big dog. When you imagine having a Mastiff, what comes to mind? Do you think of having this great grand beast to show off to friends? Do you imagine running to the park with your dog at your side, or perhaps tossing him a Frisbee on the beach? Are you finished with the dating scene and looking for a people-sized companion to keep you company? Have you had it with the neighborhood toughs threatening and vandalizing your property? Maybe you're looking for an animal that will grow up with your kids and become a fixture in the family. Are you trying to express your disgust with the neighbors small "yap" dog? Or could it be you're sublimating your true desire to a have a horse? Do you imagine working at your computer with a large sleepy beast resting against your knees?

Some Mastiffs can dwarf the people they surround!

All of these reasons, even if a little tongue-in-cheek, can be valid arguments for or against getting a Mastiff. What's important is to know yourself. Be aware, up front, of what you're looking for. Often our choice of a dog is a little like our choice of cars or friends—it springs from something deep within us. It's part of who we are. All you have to do is make sure that this is really what you want and that you are willing to persevere in the commitment.

The commitment to a Mastiff leads to the second consideration—your lifestyle. Is how you live conducive to having a large dog? Caring for a Mastiff will take a significant amount of time. Early on, your puppy will require a tremendous investment of attention, affection and socialization, and as the dog matures he will want to be around you and need exercise as well as periodic outings and trips to the vet.

The Mastiff is not a dog for the workaholic who is never home, nor is it for the person who travels frequently and will need to kennel the dog or leave him with friends. The Mastiff is for people who want to be around their dog most of the time; people who smile at the distraction of a big, cold nose rooting under their hand for attention. A Mastiff is for people who take the time to find pleasure in the unpredictable demands, mishaps, messes and surprises of sharing their home with a very large dog.

Sharing your home and life with a Mastiff brings us to the third consideration: Do you have resources to take care of a large dog? Forget the gooey stuff about how you feel—committing yourself to a Mastiff means accepting the responsibility for an animal that will depend on you for his food, shelter, health care and transportation. Such a commitment demands that you have a home big enough for the dog, yourself and whomever else you live with. Mastiffs don't do well in small, cramped spaces; they like to spread out, are not suited to climbing steep narrow stairs and they have a powerful, happy tail that can clear a coffee table in a single swipe.

Unless you want to take your Mastiff out on a leash every time nature calls, you will need a place to let him out (preferably a fenced yard). As your Mastiff will occasionally need to go to the vet and frequently go on outings with you, you'll need a vehicle big enough to transport a Mastiff safely. Finally, feeding and caring for a dog the size of a Mastiff can be a big shock to your budget. How much depends on the dog and how you choose to care for him, but Mastiffs are not for people on tight budgets. As you read through the rest of this book, the various needs of caring for a large dog will become apparent.

Give your Mastiff a fenced-in place where he can run free.

Big dogs make a big impact on an owner's life. There is little ambivalence among Mastiff owners about the importance of their dogs. Most are passionate (some would even say crazy) about their dogs. Once you decide that a big dog is for you, the future promises a great many fulfilling and exciting experiences.

Gentle Giants

Like people, every Mastiff is an individual and has his own personality, but in general, Mastiffs are gentle and reserved. With rare exceptions they are friendly, but unlike the delirious excitement of a Golden Retriever, the Mastiff is more subtle and laid-back. People sometimes mistake this characteristic for shyness, but with proper socialization the Mastiff is extremely friendly— he is just more cautious than other breeds about how and when he expresses his feelings.

Mastiffs can also be extremely stubborn. Halfway through an afternoon walk your Mastiff may decide to plunk down under a shady elm. Nothing short of dragging him with the leash will make him move. When a Mastiff decides he's had enough of a training session he will simply stop. No amount of bribing or coaxing will change his mind. While some owners find this stubbornness frustrating, most are amused and simply accept it as part of the dog's interesting personality.

Most of the time you will find the Mastiff to be an easy-going, compliant dog that loves your attention and closeness. Mastiffs love to have you home. They want to be near you and will often gently lay a head or big paw in your lap to let you know they are more important than the newspaper you are reading. Often they are content to simply lie at your feet, and perhaps even be close enough to lean against you.

In return for your attention, your Mastiff will always happily welcome you home. No matter how tough your day has been, it's hard to be depressed with 200 pounds of bark telling you how great it is to see you. A Mastiff will demonstrate endless hope and optimism and constantly remind you that you are special and important. Partially because of their size and simply because they're dogs, Mastiffs will provide hours and hours of amusement. They will make you laugh and shake your head in disbelief, and give you plenty of stories to tell your friends and family.

Not in the Lap, but Definitely in the House

Just because your Mastiff is as large as some farm animals doesn't mean that he should be in a pen. The Mastiff's need to be around people makes him a house dog. Some breeders refuse to sell to someone who plans to kennel, tie or pen the dog. If you leave a Mastiff alone or outside for an extended period of time he becomes bored, digs holes or chews on things, but most importantly he becomes depressed and anti-social. So plan for your Mastiff to be a house dog.

Fortunately, Mastiffs are fairly agreeable housemates and fairly fussy about keeping themselves clean (except for their drooling). They shed twice a year, but hair can be managed easily with frequent brushing. Most adult Mastiffs will not climb on your furniture unless you let them do so as puppies, and they can easily be taught to stay out of areas where you may not want them.

Though Mastiffs thrive in the outdoors, they still need a warm home to return to after a long day of play.

But make no mistake, a Mastiff will have an impact on your home. Your dog will take up space—lots of space. He will need a place to eat, sleep and hang out. Things will be broken or possibly chewed. And even Mastiffs, as big and powerful as they are, occasionally become ill and make messes. Food dishes will spill and mud will be tracked inside. If you find yourself easily irritated by anything that disturbs the order and cleanliness of your home, think twice before getting a Mastiff.

The Mastiff with People

Mastiffs are good natured at heart, and when properly socialized as puppies they will be fine around people. Proper socialization means providing the experience of being around and interacting with all kinds of people at an early age. But even when your Mastiff is properly socialized, don't expect him to be a glowing extrovert around other people. He will let a stranger pet him and perhaps even wag his tail, but his excitement and love will be reserved for you or whomever he spends the most time with.

Keep in mind that Mastiffs were once bred as guard dogs and by nature they are protective. Don't be surprised if your Mastiff suddenly shoulders himself between you and another person. For the dog, this is an instinctive, protective stance that he takes when something about the other person stimulates his need to be protective. Mastiffs seem to have a great internal sense about safety and danger—the best course of action is to listen to your Mastiff.

Mastiffs are also sensitive to conflict and fighting among people. If you and someone in your household are having an argument, your Mastiff may become extremely agitated and may even attempt to get between you. His understanding is instinctual rather than logical and he will simply perceive the conflict even if it's harmless and has nothing to do with him. In the same way, a Mastiff may become protective when a child is disciplined and, again, will simply want to fulfill his calling to protect.

THE MASTIFF WITH CHILDREN

With regard to temperament, Mastiffs are excellent around children, provided that they have been socialized to children as puppies. They are protective, tolerant and gentle. A Mastiff will often put up with a typical child's provoking and prodding curiosity, but you do need to be careful about the Mastiff's size. An adult Mastiff can easily knock a child down or unknowingly hit him with a happy tail. Thus it may be wise not to mix a Mastiff with children who are under the age of six. Children should be taught not to tease or roughly handle the dog.

The Mastiff and Other Dogs

Mastiffs no longer have the temperament of fighters and tend be somewhat aloof. When introduced to other dogs as a puppy, the Mastiff will generally do well. Dogs that exhibit aggression toward other dogs are usually expressing several instinctive traits. One is dominance aggression that comes from the deep instinct to establish a pecking order in the pack. When a dominant, or alpha, dog is around other dogs, he may attempt to establish himself as the lead dog. Many Mastiff owners have more than one dog without having problems, but it's usually not wise to put two alpha-type dogs together, especially if they are of the same sex.

Behavioral species aggression, in which the dog seems to be uneasy around other dogs and consequently picks fights, can stem from a lack of socialization and stimulation. It may also come from the dog's breeding or physical problems. Before purchasing a puppy, observe the temperament of the sire and dam and watch how the puppy interacts with his siblings. If a socialized dog continues to exhibit aggression, consult a professional trainer, canine behaviorist or vet. Aggression can often be curbed when its cause is understood.

Mastiffs will do just fine around other dogs if they are introduced to the idea as puppies.

The Mastiff and Cars

The problem with Mastiffs and cars is the breed's size. One Mastiff owner discovered that her puppy loved to ride in the front passenger seat of her Ford Escort, but her "boy" grew and eventually weighed over 200 pounds. She moved him to the back seat, but even there he was uncomfortable and could not turn around without getting into her space. After a near accident in which the Mastiff was flung forward during a sudden stop, she decided to find a different vehicle. A small car and a big dog are not a safe combination.

Mastiff owners need to take transportation seriously—especially if they frequently attend dog shows or go on outings. You will need a large car, a van or an enclosed pickup truck. While riding, the dog needs to have some room to move without distracting the driver and without being in danger during sudden stops. The ideal vehicle is a van in which you can fit a crate that the dog can get in or out of easily.

Barking, Biting and Chewing

A Mastiff's bark fits his size and because Mastiffs rarely bark, it is usually a wonderful sound. Of course puppies of all breeds bark, but Mastiffs seem to outgrow it and bark only when excited about your coming home or when someone suddenly rings the doorbell. If your son is learning to play the harmonica or the local fire department is testing its sirens you may hear a funny howl from your dog, but howling is not generally in their nature. A Mastiff will growl when he needs to send a warning and it's usually enough to frighten off anyone who would be foolish enough to threaten a Mastiff's territory or owners.

As for biting, a well-trained Mastiff will not bite unless he is cornered, hurt or frightened. Biting is managed during puppy training and the Mastiff should be taught that biting is never permitted. Mastiffs have powerful jaws; when they clamp down on something the force is awesome.

Chewing comes naturally to all puppies and is necessary for the development of their teeth (chew toys will be discussed further in the next chapter). Most adult Mastiffs are not prone to chew, but when they do get the urge they can do serious damage to furniture or anything that gets between their powerful jaws. When chewing becomes a problem it is usually the result of boredom or the owner not having adequately addressed the habit when the dog was a puppy.

You will discover that some Mastiffs love to dig. It's difficult to figure out what they are digging for—only rarely is it to hide a bone or even carve out a cool place to lie down—but be aware that a Mastiff can dig and once he begins, your yard may soon look like a strip mine.

The Mastiff and the Great Outdoors

While being mostly homebodies, Mastiffs do enjoy going out for walks, hikes in the woods and nice strolls through a busy park where scores of people will stop and admire their great size. The adult dog does not need a lot of exercise, but he will need to get out regularly. Owners often like to take their Mastiffs to places where the leash can be removed and the dog can move about freely. Mastiffs are not usually interested in diving into a lake, fetching sticks or catching Frisbees, but they may make a good run after a rabbit or squirrel. The important thing about taking your Mastiff on an outing is to be aware of the needs of your dog. Although they adapt well to a variety of climatic conditions, the Mastiff is not designed for extremes in temperatures, nor for running or hiking all day.

Mastiff Truths

Of course this book is biased toward Mastiffs, but there are a few truths about this breed that you need to know. First off, Mastiffs drool. Every owner learns to live with this. Of course, like Pavlov's dogs, Mastiffs don't drool all the time, only after eating and drinking, when excited or when they catch a whiff of your corned beef sandwich. And because Mastiffs like to be near you and carry their drool with them, you will

Let it be known... the Mastiff drools a great deal.

learn the word "slobber" and what it feels like. If you're smart you'll keep a towel handy to wipe the drool off after meals and drinks, because when a Mastiff shakes he can send "slingers" all over the place. "Drool" is an essential word when talking with Mastiff owners. If such things make you cringe, the Mastiff is not the dog for you.

Another truth about Mastiffs is that these big guys have a tendency to snore. The snoring results from the dog's long, soft palate that vibrates when his is breathing at rest, and produces a noise not unlike a one-cylinder tractor in a muddy field. While there is nothing you can do to change this truth, you may wish to take it into consideration when you think about where your Mastiff will sleep.

Mastiffs also pass gas. Perhaps no more than any other dog, but given their size, they have been known to send people racing from a room to fling open windows. With the proper feeding of a good quality food, unpleasant odors can be kept to a minimum.

The final truth is that none of these truths holds a candle to the joy a Mastiff may bring you. If this is the breed that calls to you and you're prepared for the responsibility of caring for a Mastiff, the effort will certainly be worth the rewards. If you are uncertain, please wait. Sadly, there are Mastiffs that are abandoned and abused because people cannot or will not care for them. Find a breeder who will let you spend a little time around the dog and talk with some people who own a member of the breed, and then make a decision when you are ready.

CHARACTERISTICS OF THE MASTIFF

Gentle

Massive

Dignified

Loyal

Protective

Sensitive

Loves to be inside
near his owners

Drool

More Information on Mastiffs
NATIONAL BREED CLUB

Mastiff Club of America
President—Joe Margraf
Corresponding Secretary—Karen McBee
Rte. 7, Box 520
Fairmont, WV 26554
email: mmcbee@access.mountain.net

Books

Baxter, Betty and David Blaxter. *The Complete Mastiff.*
New York: Howell Book House, 1993.

Moore, Marie. *The Mastiff.* Denlinger's Publishers,
1978.

Oliff, Douglas B. *The Mastiff And Bullmastiff Handbook.*
New York: Howell Book House, 1988.

Wynn, M.B. *History of The Mastiff.* Wm. Loxley and
Melton Mowbray limited edition pub. by Peregrine,
1886 (reprint 1988).

Magazine and Newsletter

MCOA Journal   Quarterly magazine; $28.00 a year. For
subscription information contact: Mary Johnson, Subscription Editor, 871 Craigville Rd., Chester, NY 10918;
email: scanner@frontiercomm.net; Internet http://
www.bigdog.geo.cornell.edu/~profiles/journal.html

The Mastiff Reporter   Bi-monthly newsletter; $10 per
year. For subscription information contact: Sharon
Krauss, 4910 E. Emile Zola Ave., Scottsdale, AZ 85254

Videos

The Mastiff   The official AKC video, available from
Direct Book Service: (800) 776-2665; email: dgctbook@
cascade.net; Internet: http://www2.dogandcatbooks.
com/directbook/

See Jane Train Spot   One hour video featuring Mastiffs
in training; to order contact: See Jane Videos, Box 555,
Eaton, IN 47448

MCOA Rescue Service

To report a Mastiff in need, contact:

MCOA Rescue
Director—Gloria Cuthbert (OH)
(216) 639-1160
email: gcuthb.aol@aol.com

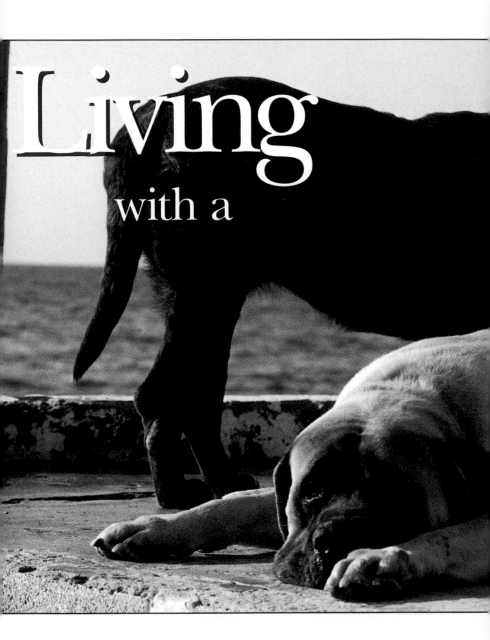

Living

with a

part two

Mastiff

chapter 4

Bringing Your
Mastiff
Home

Once ready for the commitment to a Mastiff, make one last check. Be sure that this is a stable time in your personal, family and professional life to take on a dog. Double-check to make sure that everyone in your family is in agreement about sharing their space with a dog. Finally, don't be in a hurry to make a decision. A well-bred Mastiff puppy from a reputable breeder will cost upward of $800. But even more of a factor than the money is that this is a commitment which will last eight to ten years, and one that you want to make carefully.

Now, become more specific about the Mastiff that you are looking for. Are you looking for a show dog, a particular color, a male or female? Seek out some Mastiff owners and speak with them about what might be best for your situation. Make sure you scratch a few Mastiffs' heads and take the time to imagine yourself actually living with one. Most owners like to talk about their dogs and care enough about the breed to want to help you make a good choice.

Finding a Reliable Breeder

The place to find a reliable Mastiff is from a reputable breeder who comes with high recommendations from other Mastiff owners. You can find these breeders by contacting the Mastiff Club of America (MCOA) or one of its regional clubs. The breeder should be a member of MCOA and a regional club and be willing to provide you with references. Once you contact a good breeder, don't be surprised if you have to wait

MCOA Mastiff Rescue and breeders are two great vehicles for obtaining your puppy.

for a puppy. But don't be discouraged—a waiting list is an excellent indication of the sort of dogs they produce.

One other place that you may find a dog is through the MCOA Mastiff Rescue. Rescue is a network of people who take in homeless Mastiffs and provide them with temporary homes until they can be permanently placed. The people involved with rescue are extremely careful about placement of the dogs and will help you decide if a particular dog is for you. More information on how to find reputable breeders and MCOA Rescue Service is found at the end of chapter 3.

QUESTIONS TO ASK A BREEDER

When considering a particular puppy, it's important to find out some background information about the dog. You want to know if the parents of the dog have been cleared of genetic problems. Mastiffs can have problems with hip and elbow dysplasia, eye disease, thyroid disease, heart disease and a bleeding disorder called von Willebrand's Disease. Ask if the sire and dam have been examined, tested and possibly certified to be free of genetic problems. If not, ask why, and consider finding a breeder who can assure you of the puppy's genetic soundness.

Ask the breeder why a particular sire and dam were mated. Good breeders should have solid reasons for their choice. You'll want to know what faults the sire and dam have and how the breeding sought to address those concerns. Dams should be bred neither before 22 months of age nor after 7 years of age. Make sure that you have the chance to see both the sire and dam. Ask about their pedigrees. You'll want to know if they have been shown, won any conformation or obedience titles and whether they have had any temperament training such as the C.G.C. (canine good citizen) Program.

When visiting the breeder, look for clean and supportive conditions that suggest that the dogs are well cared for. Trust your instincts. Does it seem like the breeder is caring and knowledgeable? Ask about how the puppies have been handled since birth. Have any steps been taken toward socialization? Find out how and what they have been fed. Finally, ask about the sales contract. Some of them can be quite lengthy and require the buyer to provide puppy training and spaying and neutering. Does the breeder provide any guarantee? All good breeders should be willing to guarantee their puppies to be free of genetic problems.

Don't be surprised if the breeder grills you about why you want a Mastiff and what you know about the breed. Most breeders are concerned about where they place their dogs and will want to make certain you know what you're getting into. They may ask about your experience with dogs, if you have found a vet and how you plan to care for the dog. If you are a beginner, don't be afraid to show it. Most breeders are more than willing to help you learn, and many will become valuable resources and friends as you begin your adventure with your Mastiff.

Choosing a Puppy

Having done all of the background work, it is important that you choose the right puppy. The most important aspect of choosing a puppy, after assuring her health, is studying her temperament. The temperament of each puppy is a little different, and you will want to find one that fits you and your family. Some

Choosing the right puppy for you is a difficult task, but also an extremely important one, so take the time to make the right choice!

breeders are skilled in Puppy Aptitude Testing, a process that looks at both the puppy and the buyer to make sure they "fit" together. If the breeder has this skill, let her help you choose a puppy. Even if Puppy Aptitude Testing is not available, let your breeder help you with the choice.

In choosing a puppy, you want one that fits your personality and lifestyle. If you are outgoing, assertive and have a loud and large family, you will want a puppy that is outgoing and can hold her own with her new "litter mates." If you are more laid-back, have a quiet lifestyle and are uncomfortable being assertive, you may want a puppy that is easygoing and not necessarily the leader or most assertive member of the litter.

Take your time with this decision. It may be a good idea to pay several visits to the breeder and spend some time with the puppy you are choosing. Most breeders will offer their opinion and often have valuable experience in knowing what makes a good match. Most of all, follow your heart and look for the dog that you are prepared to accept into your family. Don't accept a dog

that you are not excited about—this is one purchase
you should not make unless your whole heart says
"yes."

Puppy Preparations

Bringing a new puppy home will require some preparation. First of all, you will want to prepare yourself and
your family. Bring your puppy home on a day when you
have an adequate amount of time to spend with the
dog. Plan for a weekend or a time when you will not
be traveling or entertaining houseguests. This is a big
event for both you and your dog, and will require some
adjustment. In addition, there are a number of physical preparations you will need to make.

PUPPY-PROOFING YOUR HOME AND YARD

Just as you might child-proof your house for a 2-year-
old, you will need to do the same for a puppy. Find an
area where you will be keeping your puppy. It may not
be a good idea to give her full run of the house right
away. A room with a linoleum or tile floor works well
for the clean up of messes, and a baby gate will make a
good barrier without the pup feeling she is completely
closed off from the rest of the house. You'll become a
master at stepping over the gate.

Puppies are just discovering their new and exciting
world and will be sniffing, tasting and looking at everything. Make the puppy's area safe, again just as you
would for the 2-year-old child. Tape over electrical outlets (puppies like to lick). Remove electrical cords, rag
rugs and anything else that is chewable. Get rid of any
harmful chemicals, plants or other things that may poison the puppy.

If you plan to let the dog out into your yard without a
leash, a fence is a must. Mastiff puppies can move surprisingly fast and you don't want to be chasing them
throughout the neighborhood. Examine your fence
and make sure there are no places where the dog can
crawl through or become caught. Your yard should be
free of anything harmful to the dog such as plants like

ivy or a child's small toys. Mastiff puppies (and even some adult dogs) will eat all kinds of things including sticks, leaves, dirt and rocks. Of course, these things are everywhere, but keep the yard as free of debris as possible. Also, be sure to remove garbage cans and compost piles.

Supplies

The following are a list of supplies that you will need to keep your dog happy and in-line.

CRATE

Although not essential, a crate is an extremely useful tool for the puppy. The crate is a movable plastic and/or metal and wire enclosure that can be placed in the area where you will be keeping the puppy. A crate serves several purposes. It is a retreat where the puppy can sleep and escape children and whatever else may be going on in the house. It is also a place where you can put the puppy at night or when you are out of the house. Mastiffs do not like to soil their "dens" and will usually contain themselves while in the crate, provided that it's not for too long. Keeping the puppy in the crate at night works well in the early stages of housetraining. The crate is also useful for excursions outside the home, where the dog will need a place of her own.

Crates come in a variety of sizes and styles. Your Mastiff puppy will be growing rapidly and will eventually stand more than 3 feet tall, so buy the largest one you can find. Look for a crate that is sturdy, easy to clean and capable of withstanding heavy abuse. If you choose a wire crate, make sure the mesh is small enough to prevent the puppy from sticking her head through and possibly choking.

BED

You may like your cute Mastiff puppy to sleep on your bed, but it's not a wise idea. With puppies it's best to not start what you can't continue, and indeed there will come a day when you and your Mastiff won't fit on the bed together. Besides, as mentioned, these dogs snore. The best bed for a Mastiff puppy is her crate—some soft padding and a blanket will do fine, but choose bedding carefully. Whatever you put down is apt to become torn, shredded and possibly eaten. You'll want to replace shredded bedding immediately to prevent your puppy from choking. And don't waste your money on the soft commercial dog bed from your pet store—Mastiffs can take these apart in no time.

When bringing the puppy home, make sure she stays warm and out of cool drafts. The first few days away from Mom and the warmth of the litter may be difficult. Tucking your puppy in with a hot water bottle wrapped in a warm blanket can provide some added warmth and comfort.

Continue to provide a bed or soft rug for your Mastiff as she grows. Mastiffs have a propensity to flop down on their elbows and knees and their heavy weight can cause swelling in the joint areas. A cushioned surface can help to prevent this problem. But don't be surprised if your Mastiff wants to pick her sleeping spot. In warm weather the dog may abandon the cushions for a cool, hard surface, but it's worth attempting to move the cushions to the dog's place of choice. Arguing with a tired Mastiff is an exercise in futility.

SAFE TOYS

Mastiffs (puppies and adults) love toys and will create them out of almost anything. Because you won't want a puppy chewing on a kitchen chair, you'll need to provide some safe and appropriate toys. When confronted with the hundreds of choices in the pet store, choose toys that fit the nature, size and age of your dog. Generally you will want an assortment of toys, some for chewing, some that squeak and roll around, and toys for tugging and pulling. As your Mastiff grows, so will the toy box.

Most adult Mastiffs are not "chewers," but as puppies they will definitely need something to chomp on while working on new teeth and finding ways to expend their energy. A good toy is a sturdy, synthetic bone, usually made from an almost indestructible nylonlike substance. These come in various shapes and sizes and have a smell that dogs love. Large compressed rawhide bones are also favorites, but be careful of those that tear apart easily and become a choking hazard. Also, check with your vet. Some rawhide toys can cause intestinal problems. Others, particularly some that have been imported, have been found to be treated with toxic chemicals such as arsenic.

In general, squeaking toys and balls need to be large and sturdy enough to prevent being swallowed or lodged in the dog's throat (tennis balls are too small). Look for solid items: The squeaking mechanism can come out of a soft plastic toy and become a hazard. When introducing a new toy, watch the dog play with it. If she immediately begins to tear the toy apart, take it away. As time goes on you will discover which toys your dog likes, as well as which are suitable and durable.

Some of the best toys are those not purchased at the pet store. Boxes, rolls of paper and large plastic milk jugs are all things that a Mastiff may enjoy playing with. Just remember, a Mastiff may ingest anything you give her. Remove staples, tape or small caps before adding items to the toy box.

Bones from the butcher shop are generally not advised because they can splinter apart and lead to choking or injury. Given the many safe chew toys available today, there is no need to provide your dog with bones.

PRACTICAL DOG DISHES

A puppy needs at least two sturdy bowls—one for food and one for water. Don't get the cute ones that have two bowls attached together. You won't be able to wash them separately and food will always get into the water. Bowls will need to be appropriate to the dog's size. For the puppy, a small several-quart size is fine, but as your Mastiff grows, you will need as big a water dish as you can find, and at least a 5-quart bowl for food. Heavy plastic will do, but stainless steel is optimal. It can't be chewed, cleans up well in the dishwasher and can be sterilized. Make sure that the bowls have a wide base and are weighted on the bottom—this will save you from spills.

Speaking of spills, Mastiffs are *not* the world's neatest eaters and drinkers. They often slop things out of their bowls and they will *always* drool. A plastic tray used to park wet boots makes a great catch for messes around the food and water bowls.

LEASH AND COLLAR

A leash and collar are essential to purchase before bringing your puppy home. Even if you have a fenced-in yard, you will want to walk your dog and take her places. Don't scrimp on these items because they will see plenty of use and need to do the job without any failure.

For the puppy, any flat type of buckle collar made from sturdy soft, leather or a synthetic material will be suitable. Mastiffs have thick necks, so make sure that the collar is loose enough to be comfortable but will

Collars come in all sizes and styles.

not slip over the head. It will need to have a lot of adjustment holes to expand as your puppy grows and eventually you will need progressively larger collars.

Never use a choke chain on a puppy. Eventually you will use a choke chain for obedience training as the dog gets older. If you have never used a choke chain, consult your obedience instructor on how to fit one and how to use it. Choke chains should never be left on the dog when training sessions are over. Many people remove all collars when the dog is in the house, crate or playing in an enclosed yard. Collars can be snagged and catch on things, creating a potentially disastrous situation.

Along with the collar you will need a leash. A 6-foot leash should be plenty long. Make sure it is well made with a sturdy "catch." There will be times when you and your Mastiff will want to go in different directions. Remember there's a Mastiff on the other end. If you want to give your dog more running room, you can try one of the popular retractable leashes. But again, make sure it is sturdy enough to handle this big dog.

Although Mastiffs are still fairly unique dogs, and large enough to attract a lot of attention, they can still become lost. Never leave the house without some identification on your dog—most local governments require it. A tag, or some sort of identifier on the collar, is common. Because dogs get lost with some frequency, the American Kennel Club may soon require that all registered dogs have some sort of permanent identification. Tattooing on the inside flank or inside the ear is becoming common, and some people are even beginning to use the implantation of a tiny microchip inside the dog. These chips help with identification and keep breeders from falsifying records. Talk with your breeder about the best way to identify your dog in order to be safe and in accordance with local laws.

OTHER SUPPLIES

Other supplies you will want to have on hand for the puppy include food (see chapter 5), grooming supplies (see chapter 6) and some general "clean-up" items. A collection of old towels and rags is essential for drool, spills, mud and accidents. Be prepared to clean up around your puppy's area with your favorite cleaners, but be sure to use products that are puppy safe. You will also need items for "poop" duty. Depending on where your dog does her business, this will help you to maintain good relationships with your neighbors. Supplies include baggies and disposable gloves or one of the commercial pooper-scoopers on a stick.

Socializing Your Puppy—Giving and Receiving Love

When the exciting day arrives and the puppy is brought home, it's time to begin the puppy's socialization. Spend time with the dog. Hold her, pet her, talk to her and accept that it may be awkward at first. You may not get much sleep the first few nights, but your puppy will still need lots of sleep. Let the new puppy sleep as much as she wants and be patient. There will be an adjustment period, accidents will happen and you will both need some time to figure out how to live with each other. Your puppy will need exercise, but most of this exercise will come from play. Mastiffs should not be over-exercised as puppies (especially during growth periods) because of their susceptibility to joint injuries.

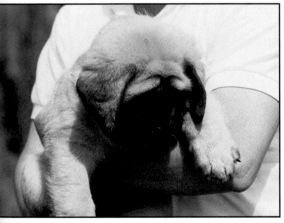

Start cultivating good habits in your dog from the start.

In addition to your attention, young Mastiffs need exposure to a variety of experiences. Not only do they need to spend time in their new home, they also need to be introduced to their world. Take them places. Let them be fussed over by other people. Introduce them to other dogs. Show them all kinds of objects. Take them for car rides and let them experience noises, smells and anything that is part of their world. Puppies are curious about everything and you will help them develop into fine dogs by investing in their socialization at this stage.

GOOD HABITS

Develop good habits in your dog from the start. Begin by introducing consistent routines to your puppy. This means feeding her at the same times, taking her out immediately after meals and letting her nap at certain times. While dogs can't read an analog clock, they have a keen sense of time. They will know when it's time for the kids to come home from school and when it's time for food. Help them adjust by introducing a routine.

Puppies are small, warm and cute and it's easy to allow them to do things you would not want an adult dog to do. Don't permit the puppy to do things you will later restrict. If there is a place in the house that will be off limits, make it off limits right away. If you don't want your 200-pound Mastiff on the couch, don't let her up there as a puppy.

GETTING HELP

Along with the joy of bringing a new puppy home, the experience can also be confusing, tiring and frustrating. You will need a support system, especially if you have never owned a Mastiff. Before you actually bring your dog home, identify some resources you can turn to when that new puppy leaves you wondering if you've

There are many information resources for lovers of the breed.

made a good choice. Those helpers may include your breeder, vet or other Mastiff owners. Another place to identify resources is your regional Mastiff club. Finally, one of the best resources for help and fun is the active Mastiff chat groups on-line. Simply search for Mastiffs on

the Internet and you'll be surprised at how many fun and helpful Mastiff people there are who love to talk about their pups and understand exactly what it's like to have a new Mastiff puppy.

chapter 5

Feeding
Your
Mastiff

When asking a proud Mastiff owner what his dog eats, you may hear the facetious response— "anything he wants!" But the truth is, your Mastiff will eat anything you feed him, and it's up to you to make sure that he gets what he needs. It's easy to assume that a dog the size of a Mastiff is a maintenance-free eating machine that only requires food in great quantity, but nothing could be further from the truth. One of the most important aspects of taking care of your Mastiff is feeding him properly.

Actually, many dogs will eat almost anything, in part because they have a rather poor sense of taste. Consequently, people often allow their dogs to eat too much of the wrong thing. Many dogs are bored and for them mealtime is a great relief. It's estimated that one out of every three dogs is overweight—and in canines, obesity can lead to all kinds of health problems. Furthermore, *what* you feed is as important as *how much* you feed.

Dog Nutrition—The Basics

Dog nutrition is a complicated science. Thankfully, there are experts who spend their lives figuring out exactly what nourishment dogs need and how to make foods that provide a balanced diet. But every dog is different and throughout his lifetime, his nutritional needs will change. Your Mastiff will count on you to be observant of his general health and feed him accordingly. Although you need not become an expert, you do need to grasp the basics of dog nutrition.

Your Mastiff needs six essential staples in his diet everyday. These staples are protein, carbohydrates, minerals, vitamins, fats and water. Good nutrition requires an understanding of what these staples are, what foods provide them and most importantly, how to balance them properly.

PROTEIN

Protein builds bones, repairs tissues and maintains your dog's growth, but protein is not stored in the body and needs to be replaced everyday. Some common sources are meat, fish, milk and eggs. The result of insufficient protein is slow growth and weak or malformed bones. Too much protein leads to obesity, brittle bones and in the Mastiff, a growth rate that leads to numerous problems. Many dog foods boast of their high level of protein. But keep in mind, too much protein is not good for your Mastiff.

CARBOHYDRATES

Carbohydrates provide your dog with energy and are a source of bulk in his diet. They also help regulate digestion and elimination. Carbohydrates come from cereals, rice, pasta, beet pulp and potatoes and break down into starches and sugars. They can be stored in the body for future use. Too many carbohydrates can lead to obesity. Not enough carbohydrates can result in a lack of energy and can lead to fertility and whelping problems.

FATS

Fats give your Mastiff's coat its shine and keep his skin healthy. They are found in animal and vegetable fats and oils. Fats also provide energy and aid in various metabolic processes. Of course, we all know that too much fat is not good for your dog and leads to obesity, but too little fat can lead to a dull and lifeless coat as well as internal problems. A balance is essential.

Fats keep your dog's coat looking healthy.

VITAMINS

Vitamins help release the nutrients of foods and are necessary for many cellular and hormonal functions in the body. The dog's body cannot synthesize most vitamins and therefore they must be acquired from his diet. If you are using a good, complete dog food, vitamin supplements will probably not be needed. It is important, however, to have a general knowledge of how vitamins affect dogs and to be alert for deficiencies.

Vitamin A

Vitamin A protects your dog's skin and is essential for a rich, shiny coat because it helps the dog's body absorb fat. Vitamin A also promotes bone growth, helps regulate the dog's growth rate, affects reproduction, strengthens the teeth and contributes to good eyesight. A shortage can lead to numerous eye problems.

The B Vitamins

The B vitamins are important to the dog's metabolism and promote healthy skin, a good appetite and growth. Indirectly, the B vitamins are critical to almost every part of the body and come from a variety of food sources, again illustrating the importance of a balanced diet.

Vitamin C

Vitamin C, the vitamin we wolf down when fighting a cold, plays a similar role for your Mastiff by boosting his immune system and improving his healing abilities. Dogs can synthesize this vitamin in their livers so you may not find it listed as an ingredient in commercial dog foods. Nonetheless, some breeders add it to their feedings, believing that it helps in fighting injuries, hip dysplasia and infections. Again, it's always best to consult your vet before supplementing your dog's diet.

Vitamin D

Vitamin D, the one we soak up on a sunny day, is good for healthy bones and teeth. Note that vitamin D needs to be consumed in conjunction with the minerals calcium and phosphorous in order to benefit the dog.

Vitamin E

Vitamin E contributes to the proper functioning of the internal and reproductive organs, as well as the muscles. Cereals, green vegetables and cheese are all good sources of vitamin E, and a shortage of vitamin E can result in muscle weakness and infertility.

Vitamin K

Vitamin K is important to the normal clotting of blood. This vitamin is synthesized in the digestive system and a deficiency is rarely a problem. However, if your dog seems to bleed for a long time after sustaining a small cut, it might suggest a lack of vitamin K—or even a more serious problem.

MINERALS

Minerals are necessary for the proper function of all the body's cellular activity, contributing to bones, muscles, cells, nerves and blood. Therefore, they are essential to general health. Two important minerals for the young Mastiff are calcium and phosphorus. These minerals need to be present in an appropriate ratio to each other to provide your puppy protection from deformities to the bones and muscles. These minerals are also important to lactating bitches. Potassium is an important mineral for normal growth and for maintaining healthy nerves and muscles. Other minerals that need to be present in your dog's diet are sodium, chlorine, magnesium, iron, iodine, copper, cobalt, manganese and zinc.

Mineral and Vitamin Supplements

Minerals and vitamins are an important component of our human nutritional needs. One of the ways we ensure that we are getting enough of them is to take a handful of vitamins and mineral supplements with our breakfast. We think that if this is good for us, it must be good for dogs. Well, not necessarily. There are numerous nutritional supplements on the market for dogs but there is no need for them if you are feeding a good-quality, complete food and your dog is healthy. An excess of vitamins and minerals, particularly vitamins A and D, calcium and phosphorous can all be potentially harmful to your dog. Consult your vet and only use supplements when you are confident that your dog needs them.

WATER

If your Mastiff could tell you what he needs most, he might say that he needs more petting and a few of those peanut butter cookies you're eating. What your

Mastiff needs more than anything else is water. Water is perhaps the most important nutrient of all. Dogs lose water through panting, urine, feces, drooling and to a limited extent, through their paw pads. While a Mastiff can go without food for days, he is susceptible to dehydration within hours of not having access to water. Dehydration should always be a concern (especially for puppies), because it can rapidly lead to numerous health problems, including death. Every cell in your dog's body needs a fresh supply of water—this is the one nutrient of which your dog can have as much as he wants.

Keep a clean and constant supply of water available for your dog at all times. Fill the water dish to the same level every day and keep track of your Mastiff's water intake. As already mentioned, Mastiffs drool when drinking, and when the water dish begins to collect drool they may not drink. Change the water and clean the water dish daily, if not more often. When on an outing, bring along a supply of water and something for your dog to drink from. Don't let your dog drink from streams and mud puddles because of the high risk of contracting disease.

What Dogs Eat

Since you won't be sending your Mastiff out to hunt, you'll have to provide all of the nutrients mentioned in some other way. You could go shopping every day and put meals together that contain all of the food groups, but that could involve a lot of head scratching and a pile of time. The alternative is to use one of the "complete" commercial dog foods that provide your dog with all the staples mentioned above.

Actually, the science of dog nutrition and the development of commercial dog food has come a long way in blending together a dog's needs into a single product. Feeding can become fairly easy, provided that you understand what your Mastiff needs, read the labels, select a proven "complete" food and pay attention to your dog's condition.

RAP ABOUT COMMERCIAL DOG FOOD

Commercial dog food is prepared in three basic types: canned, dry and semi-moist. Dry food, made up of grains, dehydrated meats and other foods, comes in a variety of preparations. In the meal form, the dry ingredients are simply mixed together. In biscuit form or "kibble," the meal is formed into bite-size shapes by adding water and flour to the dry ingredients and baking the mixture into bite-size pieces. Another type is pelleted feed in which the meal is compressed together into pellets.

Dry food also comes in a variety of flavors, sizes and shapes, and meets varying nutritional needs. Most are designed to be moistened with water before feeding. Some form a gravy when moistened and others simply soften and expand. Dry food is perhaps the most popular commercial dog food because it is easy to feed, doesn't spoil easily and is the most economical of the three types.

Canned or moist dog food is made up of a mixture of meats, grains, additives and water. Canned food will have a variety of tasty flavors, textures and contents. To the uninformed buyer, this may seem like a more nutritious meal for the dog. But in reality, depending on the product, canned dog food may be less nutritious than the "complete" dry food.

Semi-moist dog food comes conveniently packaged in nice cellophane serving sizes and is designed to look, smell and taste palatable. These heavily marketed foods contain many of the same ingredients as dry and canned food, but without as much moisture. Unfortunately semi-moist food often has a high content of salt, sugar, dyes and preservatives.

Your Mastiff can eat any of the three foods provided that the ingredients provide him with a complete, balanced diet. Many Mastiff owners use mainly dry food (moistened with water) and occasionally supplement with some canned food for the taste and pleasure of the dog.

Sorting through all the brands and types of food can be confusing, and this is where reading the labels becomes important. Look for a label that says the food is "complete" or contains "100 percent of daily nutritional requirements." Pay attention to what kind of dog the label indicates the food is for—puppies, active growing dogs or mature or older dogs. You won't necessarily want to buy according to what sort of dog the manufacturer says the food is for, but it will give you some clues. Puppy food is usually very high in protein. Food for mature dogs will have less protein and perhaps more bulk.

Check out the list of ingredients and look for meat and grains at the beginning of the list. Then look further for the percentages of protein, fat and other nutrients discussed above. Finally, don't pay too much attention to price. You don't want the generic bargain-basement brand, but neither do you have to pay designer prices. You want a food that meets your dog's nutritional and digestive needs and doesn't require a chef's kitchen to prepare.

FEEDING YOUR PUPPY

The best initial information on feeding your puppy will come from the breeder before you take your dog home. The breeder should provide you with a written description of what and how often the puppy has been fed. Don't change the puppy's food immediately. Puppies have sensitive stomachs and the upset of leaving the litter and moving into a new environment is enough stress for the dog.

The most important factor in feeding your Mastiff puppy is to understand that Mastiffs grow very fast and, if given too much protein, they can develop health problems, including joint, tendon and ligament problems. The puppy should grow no faster than his natural genetic makeup allows. Slow growth in Mastiffs is good. Too much protein and fat and too many calories may accelerate growth, but in the long run the dog will suffer numerous problems. Therefore, it's best to stay away from puppy food for the Mastiff.

A good "complete" dry or "kibble" adult dog food with a protein content no higher than 22 percent should be sufficient for a puppy. Follow the recommendations on the label for the amount that should be allotted in accordance with the weight of the dog and adjust this amount to the puppy's health and development.

Slightly moisten dry dog food before feeding and feed three times a day until the puppy is 3 or 4 months old, and then move to two feedings per day.

Finally, don't get into the habit of wanting to make your puppy happy by giving him extra treats. If your puppy has been fed properly and still seems to need something, provide him with more attention, not food. Lavishing your puppy with more treats will not make him like you more, nor will it make him happier. Proper feeding and slow growth are essential at this stage of development. As you learn to manage your puppy's diet, talk with your vet, breeder and others with reliable Mastiff experience.

Puppies have special feeding requirements.

FEEDING THE ADULT MASTIFF

The adult Mastiff will do well on a "complete" dry dog food, provided it is of a good quality and fed according to the size chart on the package. The food you choose should be in the protein range of 20 to 25 percent with fat in the range of 12 to 18 percent. The food should also be high in iodine (3 to 5 percent) and balanced for calcium and phosphorus. Some people augment dry dog food with a small amount of canned or semi-moist food, but it's important to recognize that a complete food should be all that your dog needs.

Because of a tendency toward bloat in Mastiffs, it's always best to lightly moisten dry dog food and feed it twice a day instead of in one meal. This is thought to aid in digestion and keep the dog from bolting too much food at once. To further guard against bloat some owners add digestive enzymes to their food, but it's best to do this after consultation with your vet.

The test of whether your dog is getting what he needs will be the dog himself. You want a fit dog, one that radiates health, has a good shine to his coat and has no trace of obesity. Make sure you can easily feel his ribs or see the last two ribs. If you notice significant weight gain, you may want to cut his food by a third until his weight stabilizes.

If your dog seems to be losing weight, increase the amount of food slightly, but at the same time look for signs of disease or parasites and make an appointment with your vet. Simply loading the dog up with food to help gain weight is not recommended.

As your dog ages, he will need less food. Metabolism slows down as the years go by, and the teeth and gums begin to deteriorate. In addition to providing smaller quantities of food, you may need to add more moisture to make food easier to swallow.

If your dog leaves his food without eating, don't leave it there all day. The dog may not be hungry or may not be feeling well, but spoilage can be a problem if food sits around. Always keep food dishes clean to prevent the growth of disease-producing bacteria and micro-organisms. If you change dog food (something you don't want to do often or without good reason) and the dog will not eat, continue to set out fresh food at the appropriate meal time—eventually he will become hungry enough to give it a try.

RAISED FOOD BOWLS

The Mastiff is such a large dog that reaching down to floor level to eat places the path to the stomach at an awkward angle. Some believe this angle can contribute to indigestion and the ingestion of air. Some also believe that reaching down may have some connection to bloating. Elevate your Mastiff's bowl to a height of about 12 inches for the adult and appropriately lower for the puppy.

chapter 6

Grooming
Your
Mastiff

Compared to other breeds, Mastiffs are easy to keep clean and looking good. In the grooming department they are "low maintenance" dogs. They have no fancy hairdos, and they do not need bows or ribbons. But Mastiffs do require your attention in the areas of coat grooming, toenail clipping, foot care, tooth cleaning and eye and ear care, and because of their size, these tasks can present challenges much different from grooming a small dog.

You will be sharing your home with your Mastiff, so keeping her clean and smelling good is an important part of maintaining domestic tranquillity. But good hygiene is also one of the ways to help your dog be more comfortable. As you will learn in the next chapter, many common maladies that afflict dogs (and make life unpleasant) can be limited through cleanliness and hygiene. This chapter will give you the basics for the everyday wash and wear of your dog.

Good Grooming Habits and Manners

Like little kids who don't enjoy taking a bath or scrubbing behind their ears, big Mastiff boys and girls may not understand the importance of your grooming efforts. Therefore, it's important to begin earning your dog's cooperation in grooming while she's still a puppy. Start developing good grooming habits and manners early by taking the puppy through the process and getting her used to being handled in such a manner. The dog needs to learn that you will never intentionally hurt her and that certain uncomfortable procedures are necessary and demand her cooperation.

Choose a convenient spot where you will do regular grooming. Some people place the dog on a table, but given the Mastiff's size, a low platform, or even the floor, may work fine (provided that you have good knees). Start by brushing your dog daily while she is still a puppy. Firmly, but gently, help her understand that she is to stand still and not bite. Brush gently while saying comforting words. Tell her that everything is all right, and that she's a good dog. Acquaint the dog with having you examine her ears, eyes, feet, mouth and teeth.

While introducing the dog to brushing, introduce her to having you look in her ears and check her eyes, feet and teeth. At first, don't try to do any cleaning or grooming; just acquaint the dog with your touching, looking and feeling. If a 50-pound puppy becomes used to having her jaws opened and her teeth examined, she will be much more cooperative when she is a 200-pound adult.

Make the process similar every day and be firm in your mind on how you want the dog to perform. But also, be patient. Puppies tend to think that everything is a game, and they will want to play and jump around, but persist in showing them over and over what grooming is all about, and eventually they will cooperate.

MASTIFF COAT CARE

The Mastiff's coat is not only her one and only all-purpose clothing, it's also a barometer of her health. A healthy coat appears full and rich and has a glossy shine. It will feel soft and pliable. A coat that appears dull, lifeless and feels dry and brittle can be the signal of poor grooming, but it can also signal poor diet or more serious health problems. Unable to talk, the Mastiff will tell you a lot through her coat.

*Regular groom-
ing will keep
your dog looking
her best.*

Your Mastiff's short coat will require daily upkeep and care. Like any piece of clothing, coats pick up dirt from the environment and need cleaning and maintenance. Mastiffs usually shed twice a year, in the spring and fall. Your dog and the climate will determine how significant the shedding will be, but regardless of the severity, shedding can be a nuisance to both you and the dog. The dog will itch terribly and you will find hair everywhere you go. Giving some attention to the coat everyday will greatly improve both—the dog will itch less and you will be able to collect and contain some of the stray hairs.

DAILY ONCE-OVER

Find a time every day to take your dog to the place where you will do her grooming. Plan to spend about ten to fifteen minutes brushing your dog and giving her a "head to toe" or "daily once-over." Not only will this help maintain your Mastiff's great looks, it will also give you a chance to spend focused time with the dog. This is a good opportunity to look your dog over and make sure there are no cuts, bumps or lumps that could signal other problems. Done regularly, your dog will come to expect this daily ritual.

Have the dog stand still on the grooming platform (some Mastiffs think it's a massage and want to lay down). Using a curry brush that is firm but will not scratch the skin, begin brushing the dog, starting at the head. Work around the head, pausing to check the ears, eyes and mouth, and then move down the neck. Brush with the grain of the hair, always working from the top toward the bottom to keep loose hair working down. As you brush over her entire body, use your hands as well to feel beneath the coat for anything unusual.

An active Mastiff can get pretty messy, so frequent grooming is essential.

When a dog is shedding, it's useful to first comb through her hair against the grain, performing a scratching kind of motion with your fingers to loosen the dead hair in the undercoat. Then, brush with more of a circular motion to get the shed hair out. Mastiffs are usually diligent about keeping themselves clean, but they can't reach every part of their bodies. As you are brushing, you can "spot clean" areas with a wet towel. After brushing, wiping the coat with a damp chamois cloth will remove dust and loosened hair and leave the coat looking shiny and clean.

THE OCCASIONAL BATH OR SHOWER

By faithfully doing the "daily once-over," your Mastiff will need very few baths. Frequent bathing, even with mild shampoo, can take oil out of the dog's coat. The oil gives the coat its natural healthy shine and is the substance that gives the coat its great protective quality. So limit bathing to when the dog absolutely needs it, such as when the dog smells bad, has rolled in mud or manure or needs a flea treatment. Some Mastiff owners suggest that an annual bath is plenty. Puppies should not be bathed until they are at least 6 weeks of age and have had their immunizations.

So how do you bathe a Mastiff? It's more like washing a car than giving a bath. It can be done in a large bathtub, but the whole bathroom is going to get wet, so most people prefer the shower approach outside on a patio in warm weather. It's always important to make sure that the dog stays warm. Getting a cold shower can be dangerous to her health and make her hate what could otherwise be a fairly pleasant experience.

Don't use a cold water hose. Water should be warm, at least 93°F, and the air temperature should be at least 70°F.

Before you bathe a Mastiff, prepare yourself to get wet. When a Mastiff shakes, everything around her gets a shower. Use a mild, nonalkaline shampoo. If your dog has fleas or ticks, check with your vet about the right shampoo to use. Some flea shampoos contain toxic substances, and whatever is on your Mastiff's coat will wind up being ingested when she licks it off.

Wet the dog down thoroughly, then work the shampoo into a good lather and into the undercoat with your fingers. Try not to get shampoo into the eyes, ears or nose. Let the lather sit for a moment and then rinse thoroughly. Make sure you rinse all of the shampoo out. Some shampoos suggest repeating the process, which may be necessary if the dog is very dirty.

Once she is completely rinsed, allow the dog to shake a couple of times and then towel her dry. If the weather is warm, you can let the dog run around until she is dry. Mastiffs seem to get quite frisky after a bath and will want to cavort around, but be careful. They also like to roll in the grass or dirt after a bath in order to get the smell of the shampoo out of their skin. If the weather is cold and the dog will tolerate the noise, a blow dryer can be used (provided that the dryer is not too hot). Once the dog is dry, brush her again to remove any loose hair.

Care for Eyes and Ears

Mastiffs have folds of skin around the eyes that can collect dried secretions that need to be cleaned away. Use a tissue or a moist gauze pad and gently wipe these secretions down and away from the eyes. If there is

The folds around the Mastiff's eyes collect dried secretions, which must be cleaned away.

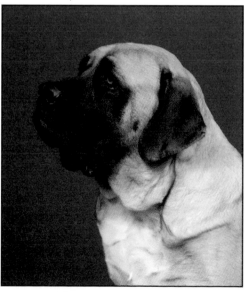

excess tearing, or the eyes are inflamed or bloodshot, consult your vet.

The downward hanging ears of the Mastiff protect the inner ear, thereby keeping the breed fairly free of ear problems. But ears will still require an occasional cleaning of the inside flap, as they collect dirt, foreign objects, ticks and ear wax. Using a damp cloth or moistened cotton swab, wipe out the outer folds and crevices of the ear. The dark-colored wax is normal and should be cleaned away. Do not place the swab in the inner ear canal. An offensive smell from the ear, or the presence of dry bloody spots, may signal problems and your vet should be consulted. If the dog is continually scratching at her ears or shaking her head violently, she may have ear mites. Ear mites are tiny spiderlike creatures that live in the deep canals of the dog's ears and cause great irritation. Treatment involves the administration of drops from your vet and is usually very effective. If not treated, ear mites can lead to infections.

Care for Toenails and Pads

Unfortunately, dogs cannot trim their own toenails or claws. In the wild, they wear their nails down through constant running and use. Unless your dog does extensive walking or running you will need to occasionally trim these big nails. Untrimmed nails can become ingrown and lead to splayed feet and slipping on smooth surfaces. Untrimmed dew claws (the claw higher on the dog's foot that does not touch the ground) can be dangerous because they can catch on collars and other items, leading to an injury.

Except for the very tip, claws are "alive," meaning they contain blood vessels and nerves. Therefore, trimming must be done with extreme care. Many owners are uncomfortable with this procedure. You may not want to do it, or at least will want to have someone with experience show you how the first time.

THE BASICS

You will need a sharp claw clipper; there are several types. In one type, you insert the claw and an angled blade is pushed down to clip off the claw. Another type is claw scissors that look similar to a refined pair of wire cutters. A more expensive tool (and actually not a clipper) is an electric nail grinder that actually files down the nail. All of these will do the job, but most people prefer the scissors.

Make sure that the dog is comfortable. Firmly holding the paw, use your fingers to extend the claw and then carefully clip off only the tip. The dead tip of the claw should be lighter in color and cause the dog no discomfort. If you are getting close to the quick, (the live part of the nail), you will be cutting into a sensitive

nerve and vein, and the dog will feel pain and perhaps bleed. Clip a little at a time; you can tell when you are getting close to the quick because the inside of the nail will appear pink.

The pads, or bottoms of your Mastiff's feet, carry a lot of weight and need frequent checking and occasional care. If the dog is licking or biting at the pad, however, check to see if something has become stuck between the pads such as a pebble or chewing gum. Use tweezers to remove foreign objects. In wet or cold weather, the pads may become cracked and can be treated with petroleum jelly.

The Mastiff's large paw pads should be checked regularly.

Care for Teeth and Gums

Mastiffs have few problems with their teeth. Dogs in general have much stronger teeth than people and rarely get cavities, but they do build up tartar that can lead to the inflammation of their gums. Check your dog's teeth during the "daily once-over" by lifting the lips and looking at the teeth from each side and by grasping the lower jaw in one hand and lifting the top with the other. Look for broken or missing teeth, swollen or inflamed gums and evidence of ulcerations.

Your dog will do a good job of keeping her teeth clean through chewing on biscuits and sturdy chew toys. In addition, many Mastiffs will eat fruit, and an apple will help clean the teeth and keep the dog's breath fresh. If the mouth smells particularly bad, some extra cleaning may be necessary. Using a toothbrush and a small amount of baking soda or canine toothpaste, you can brush the dog's teeth. With a Mastiff, this can create quite a mess and will not be loved by the dog. But if you persist you'll help clean the teeth and freshen the breath. If the smell remains or you notice something abnormal, such as a change in the color of your dog's gums, see your vet.

Care for the Backside

During daily grooming, examine your dog's genitals and anus. Make sure there is no unusual discharge from the genitals. Lift the tail and check the anus for

matting, swelling or inflammation. The dog may have soiled himself and not cleaned well. Clean away any fecal matter with a damp cloth. If fecal matter consistently collects in the hair around the anus, you may want to *very* carefully trim away some of the hair.

If your dog is dragging her rear end on the ground, this is not a sign of the dog cleaning herself but a sign of clogged anal glands. Anal glands produce the potent-smelling fluid that is the dog's communication tool to other dogs (this is why dogs sniff each others' back sides).

Routinely grooming your dog will ensure that she stays both clean and healthy.

These glands can become plugged and the fluid builds up causing the dog great discomfort. Call your vet. The treatment involves expressing fluid and possibly some antibiotics.

Your Dog's Environment

A clean environment is important to the dog's comfort and her health. Many canine diseases can be controlled through scrupulous hygiene. Because Mastiffs drool, shed and are big, happy dogs that like to spread out, you will need to allot a good deal of time to picking up after them. Make sure bedding is regularly cleaned. Crates should be occasionally scrubbed or hosed down, and your dog's food dishes will need daily cleaning. And don't forget the yard. Keeping the area tidy where the dog runs, plays and does her business will help the dog stay cleaner and limit her susceptibility to diseases.

chapter 7

Keeping Your
Mastiff
Healthy

Mastiffs are generally a healthy breed and live for about 8 to 10 years. They are similar to all other dogs in terms of general health concerns, but because of their large size and genetic background, they pose some unique health concerns,

including a propensity toward bloat, various orthopedic conditions, eye disease, skin conditions and hypothyroidism. Most Mastiffs will live normal, healthy lives with only minimal health problems, but planning ahead is good for your dog's health and your peace of mind.

Inviting a Mastiff to be part of your life includes assuming the responsibility for his health—a commitment that includes knowing how to keep your Mastiff healthy and what to do if a health problem comes up. Unfortunately, we don't like to think about pets being sick or hurt. Negotiating the whole process of finding a vet and paying the bills sounds far from the enjoyment we imagined. Yet, just like your own body, a dog's body has needs and occasional problems. You are the best health advocate he will have. Your Mastiff needs you to take the lead in his health by being informed and proactive.

Finding a Vet

The time to find a competent veterinarian for your Mastiff is before you actually bring the dog home. Don't wait until you suddenly need help and are grabbing for any D.V.M. in the yellow pages. Not all vets are created equal and certainly not all of them know about Mastiffs. You will want to look for a vet who has extensive large-breed experience and is familiar with Mastiffs. When calling, ask the vet if they have ever treated a Mastiff. Ask around for recommendations. If you purchase your dog from a reputable breeder, they will have good information about area vets. You may not find a vet with Mastiff experience, but at least choose one who is willing to learn.

As you shop for a vet, call around and ask to visit their clinic. If they are unwilling to talk with a potential client, it should tell you something. You want a vet or group of vets who are customer-conscious and willing to treat you and your dog with respect. Find out how long the vet has been in practice and trust your instincts. Are they willing to act as a resource, learn and most of all, listen? Ask for references and then check them out.

After reading this chapter you will have a good idea of what's important about Mastiffs and routine dog care.

WHEN TO CALL THE VET

In any emergency situation, you should call your veterinarian immediately. You can make the difference in your dog's life by staying as calm as possible when you call and by giving the doctor or the assistant as much information as possible before you leave for the clinic. That way, the vet will be able to take immediate, specific action to remedy your dog's situation.

Emergencies include acute abdominal pain, suspected poisoning, snakebite, burns, frostbite, shock, dehydration, abnormal vomiting or bleeding and deep wounds. You are the best judge of your dog's health, as you live with and observe him every day. Don't hesitate to call your veterinarian if you suspect trouble.

Specifically, you want to know the prospective veterinarian's recommendations for routine care. Does the vet handle their own emergencies, or do they refer to an emergency animal hospital? Are they equipped to handle a dog with acute bloat? Do they have ultrasound and EKG equipment? What do they use for a hospital? Can you visit the facility and check it out? What backup response do they provide when the vet is not available? And finally, does the staff heartily enjoy what they do and show genuine interest in you and your dog?

Preventive Care

As the saying goes, an ounce of prevention is worth a pound of cure, and prevention is the best investment in your Mastiff's health. Prevention means assuring that all of your dog's proper vaccinations are up to date, scheduling regular checkups with your vet and being ever vigilant for signs of trouble. Familiarize yourself with the basics. Read this chapter carefully and continually seek information about your dog's health.

It's helpful to develop a small library of personal resources that you can turn to when concerned about some aspect of your Mastiff's health. Network with other Mastiff owners who share your concern and love of the dog, and have breed experience. You can build a network by joining a regional Mastiff club or through an on-line Mastiff chat group. Because of the Internet, more information is available about Mastiffs and Mastiff health than ever before.

One of the first lines of preventive care is your dog's vaccinations, which will prevent him from contracting certain communicable diseases. These vaccinations begin about

> ### YOUR PUPPY'S VACCINES
>
> Vaccines are given to prevent your dog from getting an infectious disease like canine distemper or rabies. Vaccines are the ultimate preventive medicine: They're given before your dog ever gets the disease so as to protect him from the disease. That's why it is necessary for your dog to be vaccinated routinely. Puppy vaccines start at 8 weeks of age for the five-in-one DHLPP vaccine and are given every three to four weeks until the puppy is 16 months old. Your veterinarian will put your puppy on a proper schedule and will remind you when to bring in your dog for shots.

*Check your
dog's teeth
frequently
and brush
them regularly.*

*Make sure your
puppy gets all of
his shots at the
right times, and
have him neu-
tered, too. These
are both preven-
tive measures that
will keep your
Mastiff in top
health for his
whole life.*

8 to 12 weeks after birth and are given for a number of different diseases. By the time you bring your
puppy home, he should already have had an initial
set of vaccinations. You will want a
written record of those shots and
to be aware of when boosters or
other shots will be needed.

Another line of defense against
health problems is an annual checkup. Every healthy dog should see the
vet annually, and older dogs (7 years
of age and more) every six months.
This visit is for a routine checkup
where the vet will look at the general condition of the
dog, examine his coat and skin, check his eyes, ears,
nose and mouth, listen to the heart and lungs, feel for
muscle or skeletal problems and make sure that there
are no internal parasites.

Finally, the best daily prevention simply involves your
personal attention to the dog's activity, appearance,
eating and elimination. Take notice of how much
water your Mastiff is drinking. Take note of the dog's
exposure to other dogs and possible disease. And daily,
examine your dog while petting him or grooming him.
Look for lumps, bumps, areas of pain and tenderness,
swelling, discharge, distention of the abdomen or anything unusual.

Spaying and Neutering

Along with the prevention mentioned above comes the decision of whether to breed your Mastiff or to spay or neuter.

There are a number of reasons that people consider breeding their Mastiff. One is that they will probably outlive their dog and would like to have another just like the one that they already have. Another reason is that they believe their "papered" dog is something special and they would do well to have a litter of registered Mastiffs to sell. Others think that the experience of having a litter of puppies will be a great educational experience for their children.

Unless you have specifically purchased the dog to breed or show, *don't* breed your dog! Breeding Mastiffs is something that should be done with extreme care and knowledge. Unless you are planning to study Mastiff breeding and learn from other breeders, there are too many risks for the amateur. In addition, there are too many unwanted pets in the world today, and you don't want to contribute to the problem. The alternative to breeding is spaying and neutering. Spaying is an operation on the female in which the uterus, tubes and ovaries are removed. The neutering operation removes the male's testicles.

ADVANTAGES OF SPAY/NEUTER

The greatest advantage of spaying (for females) or neutering (for males) your dog is that you are guaranteed your dog will not produce puppies. There are too many puppies already available for too few homes. There are other advantages as well.

ADVANTAGES OF SPAYING

No messy heats.

No "suitors" howling at your windows or waiting in your yard.

Decreased incidences of pyometra (disease of the uterus) and breast cancer.

ADVANTAGES OF NEUTERING

Lessens male aggressive and territorial behaviors, but doesn't affect the dog's personality. Behaviors are often owner-induced, so neutering is not the only answer, but it is a good start.

Prevents the need to roam in search of bitches in season.

Decreased incidences of urogenital diseases.

Your contract may obligate you to show the dog by a certain age or have him or her spayed or neutered. If you are not planning to show the dog, don't delay. Consult your vet on the right time for your dog's surgery—you'll be glad you did. There are numerous proven health benefits to spaying and neutering, such as reducing the dog's chance of developing certain cancers. There are also behavioral benefits from the hormone reduction, leaving the dog more calm, and a better companion. If you are in doubt about this decision, talk with both your breeder and veterinarian. It's an issue you will do best to decide before the purchase of your puppy and certainly before the animal's reproductive drives are mature.

Taking Care of Your Pet at Home
VITAL SIGNS

In monitoring your Mastiff's health it's useful to have concrete indicators to measure and compare against what is normal and to note changes. The easiest indicators to measure are the dog's vital signs—his temperature, pulse and respiratory rate. Any significant variance from the norm can be a sign of problems and is useful information when talking with your vet.

Run your hands regularly over your dog to feel for any injuries.

A dog's temperature is normally between 100.5°F and 102.5°F when taken rectally. You can take your dog's temperature using an ordinary rectal thermometer, lubricating the tip, gently inserting it into the rectum, and holding it there for one to two minutes. Withdraw the thermometer, wipe it off and read. Both elevated and low temperature readings could be indicative of problems.

A normal resting Mastiff pulse rate should be somewhere between 70 and 160 beats per minute. The pulse is best felt in the femoral artery, which can be found just inside the Mastiff's upper hind leg. Gently place the pads of your fingers against the inside of the leg and move them slowly back and forth until you feel the pulse. Normal resting respiratory rate is ten to thirty breaths per minute and can be counted by watching the chest rise and fall or by placing the back of your hand near the dog's nose and mouth to feel exhaled air.

GIVING MEDICATION

Occasionally, you will need to give your Mastiff medication. Pills can easily be given by hiding them in tasty food. If you need to give a pill that can't be chewed, open the dog's jaws, place the pill on the back of the dog's

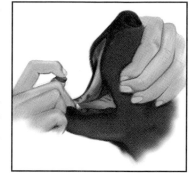

To give a pill, open the mouth wide, then drop it in the back of the throat.

tongue and immediately push it back and down with a finger. Remove your hand, quickly close the dog's jaws and gently rub the front of his neck until he swallows. Squirt liquid with a syringe into a back corner of the mouth, then close the jaws and hold the muzzle up so the liquid drains down and is swallowed.

Eye ointments are administered by carefully pulling down the eyelid, making a little pocket and then dripping the preparation into the pocket. For ear drops, turn the dog's head to the side so the opening to the inner ear is downward. Drip drops directly into the ear and continue to hold the head for a few minutes so that the

Squeeze eye ointment into the lower lid.

medication runs all the way in. As with all medications, make sure you have specific and clear directions on how to give them. If you have any doubt, call your vet—this is not the area to make mistakes.

FIRST-AID EQUIPMENT

With Mastiffs around, it's always best to keep a few first-aid supplies on hand to take care of those sudden little (and not-so-little) health problems. Create a first-aid kit for your dog with a small box, like a fishing tackle box, that you can take with you on outings. This box should include tweezers (for removing splinters, etc.), 2-to-3-foot-long narrow strips of cloth (for handling an injured dog), gauze pads, cotton balls, cotton swabs, adhesive tape, antiseptic and antibacterial ointment, germicidal soap, syrup of ipecac, a thermometer and a tarp or sturdy blanket to use if you need to move your Mastiff when he's lying down. Check with your veterinarian about the medicines and other items you should include.

From time to time your Mastiff will need to have medicine administered to him.

EMERGENCIES

In preparing for an emergency with your Mastiff, you need to know what your resources are. How can you contact your vet after hours? Where is the nearest twenty-four-hour pet emergency center? Because Mastiffs are so large, what resources do you have for moving your Mastiff should you need to get him to the vet? Answering these questions ahead of time will give you some breathing room in the actual moment of crisis.

When confronted with an emergency, quickly make sure that the dog is breathing freely. Breathing is essential to life, so do whatever you need to in order to keep the air passages clear and the dog breathing freely. Open the mouth and clear away anything that may be blocking breathing. If the dog is not breathing, you may attempt to breathe for the dog by extending the head and blowing into his muzzle. Try this several times to see if the dog begins breathing on his own.

Bleeding

Once you are sure the dog is breathing, control any external bleeding that you see. Bleeding is best controlled through direct pressure or the use of a pressure dressing directly over the source of the wound. Tourniquets are not recommended unless there is no other way to stop the bleeding (i.e., being alone and needing to drive the dog to the vet). Remember, if the dog has had a traumatic blow to the chest, abdomen or pelvic regions there may be internal bleeding. In this situation, take your dog to an emergency clinic immediately.

 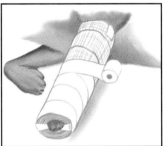

Make a temporary splint by wrapping the leg in firm casing, then bandaging it.

Fractures

The indications of a possible fracture or dislocation are swelling, deformity and pain. Some fractures will be obvious, but many times a fracture can only be confirmed in an x-ray by your vet. If you suspect a broken leg, you may want to splint the injury before moving the dog. The goal of splinting is to keep the broken ends of the bone from moving and causing more tissue damage. The splint will help minimize the dog's discomfort during the ride to the vet. You may use a splint as pictured above but you can also simply use a pillow or a blanket roll to support and stabilize the leg. Splinting should always be simple and practical. If splinting is causing extreme discomfort, just build support around the injured extremity and transport the dog to the vet.

Choking

If the dog is trying to cough or gag something out of his throat and cannot move any air, or becomes unconscious, try reaching into the dog's mouth and pulling out the obstruction. If this is unsuccessful, you can try

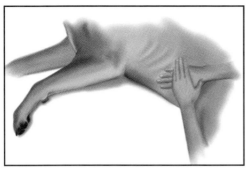

the equivalent of the Heimlich maneuver that is used on humans. Drop down beside the dog—lay him on his side, place the palms of your hands one on top the other just below the rib cage and administer several sharp inward and upward thrusts. The trapped air in the chest will create a pressure behind the obstruction when you thrust, hopefully expelling the obstruction.

Applying abdominal thrusts can save a choking dog.

Shock

All parts of your Mastiff's body, especially the brain and kidneys, require an uninterrupted supply of oxygen. Oxygen is transported throughout the body by the blood. Shock occurs when there is a general lack of adequate oxygen throughout the dog's body due to loss of blood, heart failure, dehydration or catastrophic infection. When certain organs are not supplied with enough oxygenated blood, they can be irreparably damaged and death may result. The signs of shock are lethargy; unconsciousness; labored breathing; a rapid, weak pulse; pale gums and cool extremities.

Shock is *definitely* an emergency. Keep the dog warm, don't muzzle him unless absolutely necessary and take him to a vet immediately. The treatment at your vet may include surgery, intravenous fluids and medication.

Heatstroke

Mastiffs are particularly susceptible to heat. When suffering from heatstroke, the dog's body loses its ability to regulate its temperature, and the internal temperature soars to dangerous levels. Preventing heatstroke should be a top priority in warm weather. Never leave your Mastiff enclosed in a vehicle during hot weather (even with the windows opened). Even closed buildings and apartments can become too warm on a hot day if there is not adequate air-conditioning or ventilation. Outside, in hot weather the dog must not have too much strenuous exercise or physical activity, and shade and ample water are essential.

The Signs of Heatstroke When a dog is lying down and won't get up, it may be a sign of heatstroke. He will have a weak and rapid pulse, unrelieved panting, a high internal temperature (which can be high as 109°F), pale and perhaps gray-looking gums, warm and dry skin and possibly diarrhea or vomiting. Heatstroke can rapidly be fatal if not treated. The most important treatment in heatstroke is to cool the dog immediately. Don't worry about taking a temperature. Use a hose or buckets of cold water and continue slowly cooling the dog until he improves. Once the dog is cooled, take his temperature and take him to the vet for further evaluation and treatment, which may include intravenous fluids and medication.

Being aware of your dog's health will enable him to live a long, comfortable life.

Poisoning

Mastiffs, like most breeds, are curious about everything, and so they may ingest something harmful. The problem with possible poisons is that the number of substances around today makes it impossible to list everything your Mastiff might mistake for food. If you suspect that your Mastiff may have ingested something, call the National Animal Poison Control Center. This twenty-four-hour hotline provides information about thousands of substances—which substances will hurt your dog, and what action you should take. They can be reached at 1-800-548-2423.

If your dog begins to act peculiar, consider whether he may have ingested poison. Specific symptoms are as varied as the substances out there. Some things that may indicate poisoning are vomiting, seizures, convulsions, salivation, lethargy, labored breathing and unconsciousness. If you suspect poisoning, immediately call the Animal Poison Control Center or your vet. In certain cases, they may suggest giving the dog syrup of ipecac, a substance you can purchase at the drug store and should have on hand in your first-aid kit. Ipecac will make your dog vomit soon after you administer the dosage and hopefully will help your dog get rid of any poison still left in the stomach. The vet will tell you how much to give, but generally you will be giving 2ml per kilogram (2.2 pounds) of the dog's body weight. Remember, don't give ipecac until told to do so. Certain poisons, such as petroleum products and caustic substances, can cause even more trouble when regurgitated. You may also be instructed to give the dog activated charcoal, which binds with certain poisons and keeps them from being harmful to the system.

Some of the many household substances harmful to your dog.

Potential Poisons   Houseplants, such as yew, amaryllis, nightshade, monkshood, daffodil bulbs and others, can all be poisonous. Household products, such as cleaners, paint, polish, mothballs, antifreeze and a host of other things, can be poisonous. Stow away garden products, such as fertilizers, insecticides and herbicides— these can all be killers. Keep in mind that dogs lick their coats to stay clean, so whatever substance they get on their coats will eventually end up inside of them.

Bloat and Torsion

Bloat and torsion are perhaps the most common causes of premature death in the Mastiff. These are serious and important problems that every Mastiff owner must be aware of and recognize. In bloat, the dog's stomach becomes distended with gas and air. The dog is not able to relieve the pressure and becomes extremely uncomfortable. You will notice that the dog has a large distended abdomen that is tight to the touch. The dog will be in obvious distress and may whine, salivate and try to vomit. The onset can be very rapid. Should you suspect bloat, call your vet immediately or go to the nearest emergency animal hospital.

Sometimes the distended stomach twists on axis and twists the intestine, cutting off the blood supply to the stomach. This is called torsion and often rapidly leads to shock and death if not immediately corrected. In simple bloat, the vet will pass a tube through the dog's mouth and into the stomach to release the pressure. When torsion is involved, surgery is necessary. Some veterinarians believe surgery should accompany all cases of bloat (especially in Mastiffs).

The causes of bloat are debated, but it's often associated with the rapid ingestion of large amounts of food, too much water, vigorous exercise before and after eating and feeding dry food without adding moisture. But in many cases, bloat seems to develop for no known reason. In guarding against bloat, it is advisable to feed two meals a day (so a large quantity of food is not ingested at once), limit gulping (dogs competing over the same food dish) and restrict exercise for an hour or so after eating.

A FIRST-AID KIT

Keep a canine first-aid kit on hand for general care and emergencies. Check it periodically to make sure liquids haven't spilled or dried up, and replace medications and materials after they're used. Your kit should include:

Activated charcoal tablets

Adhesive tape
(1 and 2 inches wide)

Antibacterial ointment
(for skin and eyes)

Aspirin (buffered or enteric coated, *not* Ibuprofen)

Bandages: Gauze rolls (1 and 2 inches wide) and dressing pads

Cotton balls

Diarrhea medicine

Dosing syringe

Hydrogen peroxide (3%)

Petroleum jelly

Rectal thermometer

Rubber gloves

Rubbing alcohol

Scissors

Tourniquet

Towel

Tweezers

Handling an Injured Dog

Managing a dog that has been traumatically injured can be frightening for both the owner and the pet. You will want to get the dog to the vet. But remember, the dog will be confused, frightened and in pain. Pause and assess the situation. Doing something thoughtless and reactive may make matters worse. If the dog is unable to get up or has numerous injuries, you will need a practical method of moving him.

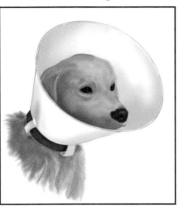

An Elizabethan collar keeps your dog from licking a fresh wound.

Before moving the dog, you will want to make sure that he is unable to bite you (the moving may be painful, causing the dog to react this way). Create a muzzle by using one of the long strips of cloth from your first-aid kit or a long stocking—wind it around his muzzle (the area in back of the nose) and tie it in a half-knot. Then pull the ends of the cloth under his muzzle and tie another knot. Finally, pull the ends back under the ears and behind the neck, and tie securely.

Weighing 200 pounds or more, an injured adult Mastiff will not be easy to move. Place a tarp or heavy blanket next to the dog and then carefully slide the dog into the middle of the tarp or blanket. With another person grasping the corners, the dog can be lifted in slinglike fashion.

Common Infectious Diseases

While fairly uncommon, your Mastiff may become infected with viral or bacterial diseases that can have grave health consequences. Having a basic knowledge of these diseases and maintaining regular immunizations will help you protect your dog from most of these infections.

CORONAVIRUS

A highly contagious gastrointestinal virus, coronavirus can be severe in young puppies. Often found around kennels and dog shows, the onset can be quite sudden and include vomiting, diarrhea, fever and depression. While rarely fatal, the disease can lead to secondary infections.

Treatment includes replacement of fluids and the administration of antibiotics (to control any secondary infections). Control is accomplished with scrupulous sanitation.

DISTEMPER

In the early stages of this often fatal systemic viral disease, the dog will appear to have a cold with a fever lasting three to six days. The dog will seem fine, but shortly thereafter another fever strikes the dog and he begins to appear very ill, becoming lethargic with a mucousy discharge from the nose and eyes. Other symptoms include gastrointestinal problems and respiratory problems, and the pads of the feet may appear thick and hard. Nervous symptoms, including seizures, spasms, paralysis and unconsciousness, may develop, and eventually the dog may die. Once infected, treatment is difficult. The good news about distemper is that the vaccine is very effective provided that the dog's shots are current.

HEPATITIS

Viral hepatitis affects the liver, pancreas and kidneys and is often fatal to young dogs. Its manifestation may not be dramatic because the symptoms are only a slight fever, lethargy and possibly jaundice (yellow discoloration of the conjunctiva and gums). Other signs include fever, rapid heartbeat, thirst, mucous discharge from eyes and nose and bloody diarrhea. Recovery from hepatitis can be slow, requiring extensive care and the use of antibiotics and blood transfusions.

INFECTIOUS TRACHEOBRONCHITIS (KENNEL COUGH)

Kennel cough is the common term for a harsh, dry, gagging cough a dog will suddenly develop when around other dogs (such as at boarding facilities and dog shows). A virus leads to an inflammation of upper respiratory passages and it may be accompanied by a slight fever. While the dog may sound severely ill, the disease usually has a short duration with treatment aimed mainly at controlling secondary infections. Puppies are usually the most severely affected and the disease is highly contagious.

LEPTOSPIROSIS

Communicable to humans as well as other dogs, leptospirosis is acquired from contact with affected urine (often that of rodents). Initial symptoms include bloody diarrhea, vomiting, fever between 103°F and 105°F, loss of appetite, jaundice and general weakness. The dog may demonstrate increased thirst as the disease progresses, and temperatures may fall to subnormal. The dog may not get up and will appear to have pain in his back and abdomen. As the disease progresses, the dog's eyes become sunken, swallowing becomes difficult and saliva may become tinged with blood. Death may result from kidney infection and failure. Leptospirosis is prevented through immunization. Treatment includes extreme care in handling body fluids, and in the administration of antibiotics and fluids.

CANINE PARVOVIRUS

Another serious and often fatal disease, canine parvovirus is a relatively new virus that is highly contagious and often afflicts an entire litter of puppies. The virus attacks the gastrointestinal tract and the heart. It is spread through contact with vomit, feces or any other discharges from an infected dog. Contaminated cages and blankets can also spread the disease. The signs include vomiting, hemorrhagic diarrhea, lethargy, dehydration, fever and sometimes sudden death. Treatment is limited to controlling secondary infections and treating symptoms as the disease runs its course. The outcome is often fatal. Parvovirus can be controlled through immunization and through good hygiene.

RABIES

This familiar disease horrifies nearly everyone who has ever been bitten by an animal. Rabies is a viral infection known in all warm-blooded animals and is almost always fatal. It is found in the saliva of the infected animal and is transmitted through a bite. The period beween infection and the onset of symptoms can be weeks or even months.

If your dog is bitten by a potentially rabid animal, wash the wound thoroughly and contact your vet. Once a dog has contracted the disease, there is nothing to be done accept to humanely euthanize the dog. The disease in dogs usually develops in three phases. The first is a change in the dog's personality in which he will withdraw and hide in dark places. The second phase is the "furious stage" in which the dog may act viciously, attack and bite. In the third stage, the dog is afflicted with paralysis and eventually dies.

The prevention for rabies is immunization and monitoring your dog's exposure to potentially rabid animals.

Intestinal Parasites

Worms and other internal parasites conjure up unpleasant thoughts. All dogs, and especially puppies, are susceptible to these uninvited guests. But fortunately, with scrupulous hygiene, the use of safe medication and regular exams, you can keep your dog clear of these pests. Your vet is a vital resource in helping diagnose parasite infections through fecal exams and advising you on which of the many medications (wormers) are safe and effective.

HOOKWORMS

Hookworms live in the small intestine and liver of the host by attaching to the intestinal wall and sucking blood. As they move from site to site they leave ulcerations that bleed. Puppies as young as 3 weeks old can have full-grown hookworms, and adults can have chronic infections without many symptoms. Hookworms are transferred through the mother's uterus and milk, through feces and through the tissue of vermin, such as rats and mice. Symptoms may be similar to those of roundworms, but with hookworms puppies can develop profound anemia from the resulting bleeding in their small intestines. Signs of the bleeding are pale gums, dark tarry stools, weakness and weight loss. Aside from ridding the dog of the worms, treatment may include blood transfusions.

ROUNDWORMS (ASCARIDS)

Roundworms are very common intestinal parasites in puppies. The tiny larvae of the roundworm can move throughout the body and can be transferred through the uterus in the pregnant bitch, through the mother's milk and through feces. Although adult dogs carry the eggs and larvae, they have an immunity to the worms maturing in the intestines. In the puppy, the larvae grow into long white intestinal worms that are often

Common internal parasites (l-r): roundworm, whipworm, tapeworm and hookworm.

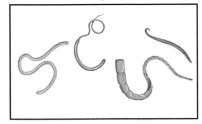

seen in the stool. A roundworm can lay 200,000 eggs daily. These are passed through the stool and can lie dormant for some time.

The signs of roundworms in the puppy are a failure to thrive, a dull, lifeless coat, a pot-bellied appearance and mucouslike diarrhea. If the larvae have migrated to the lungs, the dog may develop pneumonia. In a severe infection, the dog will vomit the worms.

TAPEWORMS

Another intestinal pest, the tapeworm is transmitted by fleas. When the dog ingests a flea, the eggs of the tapeworm develop in the intestine and grow into long, segmented worms that look like strung-together white rice. These segmented worms can reach lengths of 70 centimeters. Eggs are distributed when the segments break apart and rupture. One of the first signs of tapeworm is the ricelike segments found in the dog's stool. Other signs include lethargy, colic, mild diarrhea and loss of appetite. One of the best preventive measures for tapeworm is good flea control.

WHIPWORMS

Looking like a long, tapered, white bullwhip, whipworms live in the cecum, a pouch in the large intestine. The eggs are picked up from the environment and ingested. The eggs develop into larvae in the small intestine and then develop into adult worms. Outside, eggs can live in damp soil for years but do not survive well in a dry environment. Signs of light infections are minimal, but in severe cases there will be weight loss, a poor coat and diarrhea streaked with bright blood. Because whipworms are difficult to detect in fecal exams, repeated testing may be necessary.

COCCIDIA AND GIARDIA

Coccidia are protozoan parasites that most often come to live in a puppy's intestines. The signs of coccidia are bloody diarrhea, weight loss, dehydration and eventually weakness. The parasite is usually treated with sulfa drugs and prevention involves proper sanitation. Giardia is another protozoan that infects mammals and birds and is often transmitted through drinking contaminated water. Symptoms include chronic diarrhea, weight loss and pale feces that may contain mucous. Both of these problems can be diagnosed and treated with medication from your vet.

TREATMENT AND PREVENTION OF INTESTINAL PARASITES

If you suspect that your dog has intestinal worms, consult your vet and have the dog's feces tested. It's best not to diagnostically give the dog worm medication to see if he gets better. Find out if worms are the cause (another malady may be the cause of your dog's symptoms).

The best treatment is prevention, and most dogs will need to be on a worming program that involves giving the dog a worming preparation (syrup or tablets) on a regular basis beginning when he is a puppy and continuing every three months throughout life. There is some debate as to how often to worm your dog when he has no symptoms, so consult your vet.

Further prevention includes keeping the dog in a clean, fecal-free environment. Groom your dog regularly and clip hair away from the anus. Limit your dog's exposure to areas that may have been contaminated by other dogs and keep your dog free of fleas.

Heartworms

Unlike the intestinal worms discussed above, heartworms live in the heart muscle and can be fatal without treatment. The larvae of this killer are transmitted to the dog by the bite of an infected mosquito. As heartworms grow in the heart, cardiac and pulmonary vessels can become literally clogged with worms, causing failure in the circulatory system. Manifestations include weakness, fatigue, coughing and respiratory distress, drinking excess water, weight loss and occasionally sudden death.

Heartworms can be prevented by giving the dog a daily dose of an appropriate heartworm medication throughout mosquito season (in some climates this will be year-round). Before the dog is placed on heartworm medication, he must have a blood test to be sure he does not already have an infection. If there is an infection, the dog can usually be treated successfully.

External Parasites

FLEAS

A common, itchy affliction of dogs, this blood-sucking insect can jump great distances and readily attach itself to a host. Fleas need moisture and warmth to grow and multiply, so they may not be a problem in a cold climate. Not only are fleas irritating pests, but as already mentioned they can be an intermediate carrier of tapeworms. The problem with fleas is that they multiply rapidly and are difficult to eradicate from your dog and home. Female fleas lay eggs that drop off of a dog and then hatch into wormlike larvae. The larvae quickly grow into hopping adults that can make a home unlivable. They attach to humans, hang out in carpets and can continue to thrive even when the dog is not present.

The first evidence of fleas may be your dog's scratching. Fleas are fairly easy to see; they look like small, dark, moving specks, but you may only see small, dark fecal spots in your dog's coat—these will turn red when moistened because they contain blood. Flea bites cause local irritation, and common sites are the scrotum and under the tail—but bites can be anywhere on the dog. Some dogs are highly allergic to the saliva in flea bites and develop an angry irritation that causes intense scratching, biting and skin damage.

FIGHTING FLEAS

Remember, the fleas you see on your dog are only part of the problem—the smallest part! To rid your dog and home of fleas, you need to treat your dog *and* your home. Here's how:

• Identify where your pet(s) sleep. These are "hot spots."

• Clean your pets' bedding regularly by vacuuming and washing.

• Spray "hot spots" with a non-toxic, long-lasting flea larvicide.

• Treat outdoor "hot spots" with insecticide.

• Kill eggs on pets with a product containing insect growth regulators (IGRs).

• Kill fleas on pets per your veterinarian's recommendation.

Eliminating Fleas

Getting rid of fleas can be a real chore. You will need to treat both the dog and the surrounding environment. Flea eggs can stay in a dormant state for literally years, awaiting the perfect hatch conditions. Insecticidal shampoos work best for the dog, and sprays and foggers are used for the environment. These cures can be toxic and should be used with the advice of your vet and with extreme caution.

The flea is a die-hard pest.

TICKS

A particularly repulsive blood-sucking parasite, the tick is a hardy carrier of many diseases including Rocky Mountain spotted fever, Lyme disease, and encephalitis.

Ticks are found in tall grass and wooded areas and seem to have an uncanny ability to find dogs (and people). Tick season is anytime the temperature is above freezing. Ticks attach themselves to the dog by burying their heads into the skin and sucking blood until they become grossly bloated.

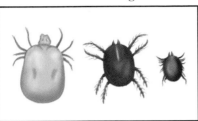

The tick-borne Lyme Disease is widespread throughout the U.S., and is best known for its severe impact on people, but it also affects dogs. It's caused by the spirochete, *Borrelia burgdorferi*, and transmitted primarily through deer ticks. The symptoms of Lyme Disease are confusing and a matter of much debate, but in general they include weakness, lethargy, fever, joint swelling and severe pain that seems to move about in the back and/or limbs. The disease is treatable by your vet. They should be aware of the extent of the problem in your area and a helpful resource when consulted about tick control.

Three types of ticks (l-r): the wood tick, brown dog tick and deer tick.

Removing Ticks

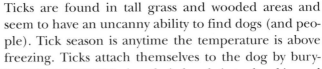

Ticks can attach anywhere, but they prefer the underside of a dog's ears. There are many myths about removing attached ticks, but the best method is to simply grasp the tick as close to its head as possible with tweezers and a gloved hand and pull it straight out. First smear petroleum jelly or drop alcohol on the tick and let it sit for a minute. Grasp the tick with the tweezers and pull firmly to remove the entire head. If the head of the tick is left burrowed in the skin, it may lead to infection and possibly abscess. Be sure to swab the area with disinfectant and check the site for infection over the next few days. Prevention includes special tick collars and sprays and checking your dog for ticks after outings. Again, check with your vet for the recommended prevention for the ticks in your area.

Use tweezers to remove ticks from your dog.

Common Medical Problems Found in the Mastiff

PROGRESSIVE RETINAL ATROPHY (PRA)

Among several hereditary eye problems with Mastiffs, the most common is Progressive Retinal Atrophy (PRA) Type I. This disease seems to be on the increase, currently has no treatment and eventually leads to complete and permanent blindness. PRA manifests itself with the early loss of night vision followed by the loss of day vision. As the disease progresses, it affects how the pupils respond to light, and in some cases the dog will develop cataracts. The problem with this disease is that it often is not diagnosed until the dog is well on his way to complete blindness. You will want to know if your dog has this disease, especially if you plan to breed him. PRA testing can be done on puppies as young as 8 weeks old. A blood test that will actually pinpoint carriers of this potentially devastating disease is currently being developed. Breeders can also certify and register Mastiffs as being clear of the disease. Ask about PRA when purchasing a puppy.

Check you Mastiff for external parasites frequently.

ELBOW AND KNEE BURSAS

If you hang around Mastiffs much, you'll notice that some have swelling and lumps around their elbows and knees. Mastiffs develop this problem because of their size and weight, and as a result of using their elbows and knees when getting up and flopping down. Bursas often come and go in puppies. The swelling is actually nature's way of protecting the joint.

Bursas start as fluid-filled pockets around the joints that eventually can develop into a pad of tissue around the joint.

The proper treatment is subject to much controversy. Some suggest surgery in the adults, but surgery always poses risks to the joint. Others believe bursas should be left alone and still others suggest a variety of potions and cures. Once again, you will want to use your vet as a resource and talk with others who are familiar with this Mastiff problem.

Hip Dysplasia

Hip dysplasia is common to all breeds, but it is of particular concern to Mastiff owners because of the dog's size and weight. The problem is a hereditary one, but it is difficult to monitor because it can skip generations. It is also believed that certain metabolic and dietary factors may play a role in this malady. In hip dysplasia, the head of femur (large thigh bone) and the acetabulum (the hip socket) become incompatible and no longer fit together, leading to lameness and arthritis. The dog will appear to be uncomfortable with strenuous activity, walk oddly, appear to be in pain, be reluctant to climb stairs and may have trouble getting up.

Hip dysplasia usually shows up when a dog is anywhere between 4 months and 1 year old, but diagnosis cannot be made with certainty without an x-ray. All Mastiffs should be x-rayed at one year of age, when hips are well formed. Not every young dog with an awkward gait should be assumed to have hip dysplasia. No Mastiff, with even mild dysplasia, should be bred. Treatment of the problem ranges from simply relieving the symptoms to, though very controversial, total hip-replacement surgery.

Hypothyroidism

Metabolism, or how energy is made available in a dog's body, is regulated by the thyroid gland. Although there is still much to be learned about metabolism and thyroid problems in large dogs, it is thought that some Mastiffs may have a genetic propensity to have a progressive loss of thyroid function that leads to a deficit in thyroid hormone secretion. This deficit is called hypothyroidism and results in a general loss of energy in the dog, increased sleeping, decreased exercise tolerance, weight gain, a dry and brittle coat, hair loss, lowered body temperature, infertility and a darker skin color. Hypothyroidism can be diagnosed with a blood test and treated with a synthetic thyroxine, but the condition is not reversible.

Old Age

Mastiffs normally live to be 8 to 10 years of age. Some die even younger if they are overweight or have other health problems. With this relatively short life span, you will want to enjoy every day with your dog, but eventually he will begin to slow down. You will begin to notice that your dog tires more easily. This is a time to honor his age and let him rest. You will need to pay more attention to your older dog's comfort. He will have difficulty climbing stairs, will be more sensitive to heat and will sleep more. He will not need as much food, but you may have to feed him more often and in smaller amounts. You should watch the weight of your Mastiff carefully as he ages and consequently burns fewer calories. He will need to consume fewer calories and protein as his activity slows down and his body changes. You will still want to keep the dog fit. Extra weight constitutes added stress on the already creaking joints.

Saying Good-Bye

Hopefully your dog will pass on while resting and without pain, but there may come a time when you need to make a decision to end the dog's suffering. If your dog is having difficulty getting up, is not eating well and is in obvious pain, you will want to think hard about the quality of his life. If you decide that the dog should be euthanized, have the vet come to your house while you hold the dog as he is put to sleep. The dog should have the last comfort of being in familiar surroundings and being held by the people he has faithfully loved.

TAKE TIME TO HEAL

Grief is a natural reaction to the loss of a pet. Give yourself time to grieve the loss of your companion. Talking to others who have lost an old dog and can relate to your loss can be especially helpful.

Your Happy, Healthy Pet

Your Dog's Name _____

Name on Your Dog's Pedigree (if your dog has one) _____

_____

Where Your Dog Came From _____

_____

Your Dog's Birthday _____

Your Dog's Veterinarian

    Name _____

    Address _____

    Phone Number_____

    Emergency Number_____

Your Dog's Health

    Vaccines

    type _____ date given _____

    type _____ date given _____

    type _____ date given _____

    type _____ date given _____

    Heartworm

    date tested _____ type used_____ start date _____

Your Dog's License Number_____

Groomer's Name and Number _____

Dogsitter/Walker's Name and Number_____

Awards Your Dog Has Won

    Award _____ date earned _____

    Award _____ date earned _____

part three

Enjoying
your
Dog

chapter 8

Basic
Training

by Ian Dunbar, Ph.D., MRCVS

Training is the jewel in the crown—the most important aspect of doggy husbandry. There is no more important variable influencing dog behavior and temperament than the dog's education: A well-trained, well-behaved and good-natured puppydog is always a joy to live with, but an untrained and uncivilized dog can be a perpetual nightmare. Moreover, deny the dog an education and she will not have the opportunity to fulfill her own canine potential; neither will she have the ability to communicate effectively with her human companions.

Luckily, modern psychological training methods are easy, efficient, effective and, above all, considerably dog-friendly and user-friendly.

Doggy education is as simple as it is enjoyable. But before you can have a good time play-training with your new dog, you have to learn what to do and how to do it. There is no bigger variable influencing the success of dog training than the *owner's* experience and expertise. *Before you embark on the dog's education, you must first educate yourself.*

Basic Training for Owners

Ideally, basic owner training should begin well *before* you select your dog. Find out all you can about your chosen breed first, then master rudimentary training and handling skills. If you already have your puppydog, owner training is a dire emergency—the clock is ticking! Especially for puppies, the first few weeks at home are the most important and influential days in the dog's life. Indeed, the cause of most adolescent and adult problems may be traced back to the initial days the pup explores her new home. This is the time to establish the *status quo*—to teach the puppydog how you would like her to behave and so prevent otherwise quite predictable problems.

In addition to consulting breeders and breed books such as this one (which understandably have a positive breed bias), seek out as many pet owners with your breed as you can find. Good points are obvious. What you want to find out are the breed-specific *problems,* so you can nip them in the bud. In particular, you should talk to owners with *adolescent* dogs and make a list of all anticipated problems. Most important, *test drive* at least half a dozen adolescent and adult dogs of your breed yourself. An 8-week-old puppy is deceptively easy to handle, but she will acquire adult size, speed and strength in just four months, so you should learn now what to prepare for.

Puppy and pet dog training classes offer a convenient venue to locate pet owners and observe dogs in action. For a list of suitable trainers in your area, contact the Association of Pet Dog Trainers (see chapter 13). You may also begin your basic owner training by observing other owners in class. Watch as many classes and test drive as many dogs as possible. Select an upbeat, dog-friendly, people-friendly, fun-and-games, puppydog pet training class to learn the ropes. Also, watch training videos and read training books. You must find out what to do and how to do it *before* you have to do it.

Principles of Training

Most people think training comprises teaching the dog to do things such as sit, speak and roll over, but even a 4-week-old pup knows how to do these things already. Instead, the first step in training involves teaching the dog human words for each dog behavior and activity and for each aspect of the dog's environment. That way you, the owner, can more easily participate in the dog's domestic education by directing her to perform specific actions appropriately, that is, at the right time, in the right place and so on. Training opens communication channels, enabling an educated dog to at least understand her owner's requests.

In addition to teaching a dog *what* we want her to do, it is also necessary to teach her *why* she should do what we ask. Indeed, 95 percent of training revolves around motivating the dog *to want to do* what we want. Dogs often understand what their owners want; they just don't see the point of doing it—especially when the owner's repetitively boring and seemingly senseless instructions are totally at odds with much more pressing and exciting doggy distractions. It is not so much the dog that is being stubborn or dominant; rather, it is the owner who has failed to acknowledge the dog's needs and feelings and to approach training from the dog's point of view.

THE MEANING OF INSTRUCTIONS

The secret to successful training is learning how to use training lures to predict or prompt specific behaviors—to coax the dog to do what you want *when* you want. Any highly valued object (such as a treat or toy) may be used as a lure, which the dog will follow with her eyes and nose. Moving the lure in specific ways entices the dog to move her nose, head and entire body in specific ways. In fact, by learning the art of manipulating various lures, it is possible to teach the dog to assume virtually any body position and perform any action. Once you have control over the expression of the dog's behaviors and can elicit any body position or behavior at will, you can easily teach the dog to perform on request.

Teach your dog words for each activity she needs to know, like down.

Tell your dog what you want her to do, use a lure to entice her to respond correctly, then profusely praise and maybe reward her once she performs the desired action. For example, verbally request "Tina, sit!" while you move a squeaky toy upwards and backwards over the dog's muzzle (lure-movement and hand signal), smile knowingly as she looks up (to follow the lure) and sits down (as a result of canine anatomical engineering), then praise her to distraction ("Gooood Tina!"). Squeak the toy, offer a training treat and give your dog and yourself a pat on the back.

Being able to elicit desired responses over and over enables the owner to reward the dog over and over. Consequently, the dog begins to think training is fun. For example, the more the dog is rewarded for sitting, the more she enjoys sitting. Eventually the dog comes to realize that, whereas most sitting is appreciated, sitting immediately upon request usually prompts especially enthusiastic praise and a slew of high-level rewards. The dog begins to sit on cue much of the time, showing that she is starting to grasp the meaning of the owner's verbal request and hand signal.

WHY COMPLY?

Most dogs enjoy initial lure-reward training and are only too happy to comply with their owners' wishes. Unfortunately, repetitive drilling without appreciative feedback tends to diminish the dog's enthusiasm until she eventually fails to see the point of complying anymore. Moreover, as the dog approaches adolescence she becomes more easily distracted as she develops other interests. Lengthy sessions with repetitive exercises tend to bore and demotivate both parties. If it's not fun, the owner doesn't do it and neither does the dog.

Integrate training into your dog's life: The greater number of training sessions each day and the *shorter* they are, the more willingly compliant your dog will

become. Make sure to have a short (just a few seconds) training interlude before every enjoyable canine activity. For example, ask your dog to sit to greet people, to sit before you throw her Frisbee and to sit for her supper. Really, sitting is no different from a canine "Please."

To train your dog, you need gentle hands, a loving heart and a good attitude.

Also, include numerous short training interludes during every enjoyable canine pastime, for example, when playing with the dog or when she is running in the park. In this fashion, doggy distractions may be effectively converted into rewards for training. Just as all games have rules, fun becomes training . . . and training becomes fun.

Eventually, rewards actually become unnecessary to continue motivating your dog. If trained with consideration and kindness, performing the desired behaviors will become self-rewarding and, in a sense, your dog will motivate herself. Just as it is not necessary to reward a human companion during an enjoyable walk in the park, or following a game of tennis, it is hardly necessary to reward our best friend—the dog—for walking by our side or while playing fetch. Human company during enjoyable activities is reward enough for most dogs.

Even though your dog has become self-motivating, it's still good to praise and pet her a lot and offer rewards once in a while, especially for a good job well done. And if for no other reason, praising and rewarding others is good for the human heart.

PUNISHMENT

Without a doubt, lure-reward training is by far the best way to teach: Entice your dog to do what you want and then reward her for doing so. Unfortunately, a human shortcoming is to take the good for granted and to moan and groan at the bad. Specifically, the dog's many good behaviors are ignored while the owner focuses on punishing the dog for making mistakes. In extreme cases, instruction is *limited* to punishing mistakes made by a trainee dog, child, employee or husband, even though it has been proven punishment training is notoriously inefficient and ineffective and is decidedly unfriendly and combative. It teaches the dog that training is a drag, almost as quickly as it teaches the dog to dislike her trainer. Why treat our best friends like our worst enemies?

Punishment training is also much more laborious and time consuming. Whereas it takes only a finite amount of time to teach a dog what to chew, for example, it takes much, much longer to punish the dog for each and every mistake. Remember, *there is only one right way!* So why not teach that right way from the outset?!

To make matters worse, punishment training causes severe lapses in the dog's reliability. Since it is obviously impossible to punish the dog each and every time she misbehaves, the dog quickly learns to distinguish between those times when she must comply (so as to avoid impending punishment) and those times when she need not comply, because punishment is impossible. Such times include when the dog is off leash and 6 feet away, when the owner is otherwise engaged (talking to a friend, watching television, taking a shower, tending to the baby or chatting on the telephone) or when the dog is left at home alone.

Instances of misbehavior will be numerous when the owner is away, because even when the dog complied in the owner's looming presence, she did so unwillingly. The dog was forced to act against her will, rather than molding her will to want to please. Hence, when the owner is absent, not only does the dog know she need not comply, she simply does not want to. Again, the trainee is not a stubborn vindictive beast, but rather the trainer has failed to teach. Punishment training invariably creates unpredictable Jekyll and Hyde behavior.

Trainer's Tools

Many training books extol the virtues of a vast array of training paraphernalia and electronic and metallic gizmos, most of which are designed for canine restraint, correction and punishment, rather than for actual facilitation of doggy education. In reality, most effective training tools are not found in stores; they come from within ourselves. In addition to a willing dog, all you really need is a functional human brain, gentle hands, a loving heart and a good attitude.

In terms of equipment, all dogs do require a quality buckle collar to sport dog tags and to attach the leash (for safety and to comply with local leash laws). Hollow chew toys (like Kongs or sterilized longbones) and a dog bed or collapsible crate are musts for housetraining. Three additional tools are required:

1. specific lures (training treats and toys) to predict and prompt specific desired behaviors;

2. rewards (praise, affection, training treats and toys) to reinforce for the dog what a lot of fun it all is; and

3. knowledge—how to convert the dog's favorite activities and games (potential distractions to training) into "life-rewards," which may be employed to facilitate training.

The most powerful of these is *knowledge*. Education is the key! Watch training classes, participate in training classes, watch videos, read books, enjoy play-training with your dog and then your dog will say "Please," and your dog will say "Thank you!"

Housetraining

If dogs were left to their own devices, certainly they would chew, dig and bark for entertainment and then no doubt highlight a few areas of their living space with sprinkles of urine, in much the same way we decorate by hanging pictures. Consequently, when we ask a dog to live with us, we must teach her *where* she may dig, *where* she may perform her toilet duties, *what* she may chew and *when* she may bark. After all, when left at home alone for many hours, we cannot expect the dog to amuse herself by completing crosswords or watching the soaps on TV!

Also, it would be decidedly unfair to keep the house rules a secret from the dog, and then get angry and punish the poor critter for inevitably transgressing rules she did not even know existed. Remember: Without adequate education and guidance, the dog will be forced to establish her own rules—doggy rules—and most probably will be at odds with the owner's view of domestic living.

Since most problems develop during the first few days the dog is at home, prospective dog owners must be certain they are quite clear about the principles of housetraining *before* they get a dog. Early misbehaviors quickly become established as the *status quo*—

becoming firmly entrenched as hard-to-break bad habits, which set the precedent for years to come. Make sure to teach your dog good habits right from the start. Good habits are just as hard to break as bad ones!

Ideally, when a new dog comes home, try to arrange for someone to be present as much as possible during the first few days (for adult dogs) or weeks for puppies. With only a little forethought, it is surprisingly easy to find a puppy sitter, such as a retired person, who would be willing to eat from your refrigerator and watch your television while keeping an eye on the newcomer to encourage the dog to play with chew toys and to ensure she goes outside on a regular basis.

POTTY TRAINING

To teach the dog where to relieve herself:

1. never let her make a single mistake;

2. let her know where you want her to go; and

3. handsomely reward her for doing so: "GOOOOOOOD DOG!!!" liver treat, liver treat, liver treat!

Preventing Mistakes

A single mistake is a training disaster, since it heralds many more in future weeks. And each time the dog soils the house, this further reinforces the dog's unfortunate preference for an indoor, carpeted toilet. *Do not let an unhousetrained dog have full run of the house.*

When you are away from home, or cannot pay full attention, confine the dog to an area where elimination is appropriate, such as an outdoor run or, better still, a small, comfortable indoor kennel with access to an outdoor run. When confined in this manner, most dogs will naturally housetrain themselves.

If that's not possible, confine the dog to an area, such as a utility room, kitchen, basement or garage, where elimination may not be desired in the long run but as an interim measure it is certainly preferable to doing it all around the house. Use newspaper to cover the floor of the dog's day room. The newspaper may be used to soak up the urine and to wrap up and dispose of the feces. Once your dog develops a preferred spot for eliminating, it is only necessary to cover that part of the floor with newspaper. The smaller papered area may then be moved (only a little each day) towards the door to the outside. Thus the dog will develop the tendency to go to the door when she needs to relieve herself.

Never confine an unhousetrained dog to a crate for long periods. Doing so would force the dog to soil the crate and ruin its usefulness as an aid for housetraining (see the following discussion).

Teaching Where

In order to teach your dog where you would like her to do her business, you have to be there to direct the proceedings—an obvious, yet often neglected, fact of life. In order to be there to teach the dog *where* to go, you need to know *when* she needs to go. Indeed, the success of housetraining depends on the owner's ability to predict these times. Certainly, a regular feeding schedule will facilitate prediction somewhat, but there is nothing like "loading the deck" and influencing the timing of the outcome yourself!

The first few weeks at home are the most important and influential in your dog's life.

Whenever you are at home, make sure the dog is under constant supervision and/or confined to a small area. If already well trained, simply instruct the dog to lie down in her bed or basket. Alternatively, confine the dog to a crate (doggy den) or tie-down (a short, 18-inch lead that can be clipped to an eye hook in the baseboard near her bed). Short-term close confinement strongly inhibits urination and defecation, since the dog does not want to soil her sleeping area. Thus, when you release the puppydog each hour, she will definitely need to urinate immediately and defecate every third or fourth hour. Keep the dog confined to her doggy den and take her to her intended toilet area each hour, every hour and on the hour.

When taking your dog outside, instruct her to sit quietly before opening the door—she will soon learn to sit by the door when she needs to go out!

Teaching Why

Being able to predict when the dog needs to go enables the owner to be on the spot to praise and reward the dog. Each hour, hurry the dog to the intended toilet area in the yard, issue the appropriate instruction ("Go pee!" or "Go poop!"), then give the dog three to four minutes to produce. Praise and offer a couple of training treats when successful. The treats are important because many people fail to praise their dogs with feeling . . . and housetraining is hardly the time for understatement. So either loosen up and enthusiastically praise that dog: "Wuzzzer-wuzzer-wuzzer, hoooser good wuffer den? Hoooo went pee for Daddy?" Or say "Good dog!" as best you can and offer the treats for effect.

Following elimination is an ideal time for a spot of play-training in the yard or house. Also, an empty dog may be allowed greater freedom around the house for the next half hour or so, just as long as you keep an eye out to make sure she does not get into other kinds of mischief. If you are preoccupied and cannot pay full attention, confine the dog to her doggy den once more to enjoy a peaceful snooze or to play with her many chew toys.

If your dog does not eliminate within the allotted time outside—no biggie! Back to her doggy den, and then try again after another hour.

As I own large dogs, I always feel more relaxed walking an empty dog, knowing that I will not need to finish our stroll weighted down with bags of feces!

Beware of falling into the trap of walking the dog to get her to eliminate. The good ol' dog walk is such an enormous highlight in the dog's life that it represents the single biggest potential reward in domestic dogdom. However, when in a hurry, or during inclement weather, many owners abruptly terminate the walk the moment the dog has done her business. This, in effect, severely punishes the dog for doing the right thing, in the right place at the right time. Consequently, many dogs become strongly inhibited from eliminating outdoors because they know it will signal an abrupt end to an otherwise thoroughly enjoyable walk.

Instead, instruct the dog to relieve herself in the yard prior to going for a walk. If you follow the above instructions, most dogs soon learn to eliminate on cue. As soon as the dog eliminates, praise (and offer a treat or two)—"Good dog! Let's go walkies!" Use the walk as a reward for eliminating in the yard. If the dog does not go, put her back in her doggy den and think about a walk later on. You will find with a "No feces—no walk" policy, your dog will become one of the fastest defecators in the business.

If you do not have a backyard, instruct the dog to eliminate right outside your front door prior to the walk. Not only will this facilitate clean up and disposal of the feces in your own trash can but, also, the walk may again be used as a colossal reward.

CHEWING AND BARKING

Short-term close confinement also teaches the dog that occasional quiet moments are a reality of domestic living. Your puppydog is extremely impressionable during her first few weeks at home. Regular confinement at this time soon exerts a calming influence over the dog's personality. Remember, once the dog is housetrained and calmer, there will be a whole lifetime ahead for the dog to enjoy full run of the house and garden. On the other hand, by letting the newcomer have unrestricted access to the entire household and allowing her to run willy-nilly, she will most certainly develop a bunch of behavior problems in short order, no doubt necessitating confinement later in life. It would not be fair to remedially restrain and confine a dog you have trained, through neglect, to run free.

When confining the dog, make sure she always has an impressive array of suitable chew toys. Kongs and sterilized longbones (both readily available from pet stores) make the best chew toys, since they are hollow and may be stuffed with treats to heighten the dog's interest. For example, by stuffing the little hole at the top of a Kong with a small piece of freeze-dried liver, the dog will not want to leave it alone.

Remember, treats do not have to be junk food and they certainly should not represent extra calories. Rather, treats should be part of each dog's regular

Make sure your puppy has suitable chew toys.

daily diet: Some food may be served in the dog's bowl for breakfast and dinner, some food may be used as training treats, and some food may be used for stuffing chew toys. I regularly stuff my dogs' many Kongs with different shaped biscuits and kibble. The kibble seems to fall out fairly easily, as do the oval-shaped biscuits, thus rewarding the dog instantaneously for checking out the chew toys. The bone-shaped biscuits fall out after a while, rewarding the dog for worrying at the chew toy. But the triangular biscuits never come out. They remain inside the Kong as lures, maintaining the dog's fascination with her chew toy. To further focus the dog's interest, I always make sure to flavor the triangular biscuits by rubbing them with a little cheese or freeze-dried liver.

To teach come, call your dog, open your arms as a welcoming signal, wave a toy or a treat and praise for every step in your direction.

If stuffed chew toys are reserved especially for times the dog is confined, the puppydog will soon learn to enjoy quiet moments in her doggy den and she will quickly develop a chew-toy habit— a good habit! This is a simple *autoshaping* process; all the owner has to do is set up the situation and the dog all but trains herself— easy and effective. Even when the dog is given run of the house, her first inclination will be to indulge her rewarding chew-toy habit rather than destroy less-attractive household articles, such as curtains, carpets, chairs and compact disks. Similarly, a chew-toy chewer will be less inclined to scratch and chew herself excessively. Also, if the dog busies herself as a recreational chewer, she will be less inclined to develop into a recreational barker or digger when left at home alone.

Stuff a number of chew toys whenever the dog is left confined and remove the extra-special-tasting treats when you return. Your dog will now amuse herself with her chew toys before falling asleep and then resume playing with her chew toys when she expects you to return. Since most owner-absent misbehavior happens right after you leave and right before your expected return, your puppydog will now be conveniently preoccupied with her chew toys at these times.

Come and Sit

Most puppies will happily approach virtually anyone, whether called or not; that is, until they collide with adolescence and

develop other more important doggy interests, such as sniffing a multiplicity of exquisite odors on the grass. Your mission, Mr./Ms. Owner, is to teach and reward the pup for coming reliably, willingly and happily when called—and you have just three months to get it done. Unless adequately reinforced, your puppy's tendency to approach people will self-destruct by adolescence.

Call your dog ("Tina, come!"), open your arms (and maybe squat down) as a welcoming signal, waggle a treat or toy as a lure and reward the puppydog when she comes running. Do not wait to praise the dog until she reaches you—she may come 95 percent of the way and then run off after some distraction. Instead, praise the dog's *first* step towards you and continue praising enthusiastically for *every* step she takes in your direction.

When the rapidly approaching puppy dog is three lengths away from impact, instruct her to sit ("Tina, sit!") and hold the lure in front of you in an outstretched hand to prevent her from hitting you mid-chest and knocking you flat on your back! As Tina decelerates to nose the lure, move the treat upwards and backwards just over her muzzle with an upwards motion of your extended arm (palm-upwards). As the dog looks up to follow the lure, she will sit down (if she jumps up, you are holding the lure too high). Praise the dog for sitting. Move backwards and call her again. Repeat this many times over, always praising when Tina comes and sits; on occasion, reward her.

For the first couple of trials, use a training treat both as a lure to entice the dog to come and sit and as a reward for doing so. Thereafter, try to use different items as lures and rewards. For example, lure the dog with a Kong or Frisbee but reward her with a food treat. Or lure the dog with a food treat but pat her and throw a tennis ball as a reward. After just a few repetitions, dispense with the lures and rewards; the dog will begin to respond willingly to your verbal requests and hand signals just for the prospect of praise from your heart and affection from your hands.

Instruct every family member, friend and visitor how to get the dog to come and sit. Invite people over for a series of pooch parties; do not keep the pup a secret—let other people enjoy this puppy, and let the pup enjoy other people. Puppydog parties are not only fun, they easily attract a lot of people to help *you* train *your* dog. Unless you teach your dog how to meet people, that is, to sit for greetings, no doubt the dog will resort to jumping up. Then you and the visitors will get annoyed, and the dog will be punished. This is not fair. *Send out those invitations for puppy parties and teach your dog to be mannerly and socially acceptable.*

Even though your dog quickly masters obedient recalls in the house, her reliability may falter when playing in the backyard or local park. Ironically, it is *the owner* who has unintentionally trained the dog *not* to respond in these instances. By allowing the dog to play and run around and otherwise have a good time, but then to call the dog to put her on leash to take her home, the dog quickly learns playing is fun but training is a drag. Thus, playing in the park becomes a severe distraction, which works against training. Bad news!

Instead, whether playing with the dog off leash or on leash, request her to come at frequent intervals—say, every minute or so. On most occasions, praise and pet the dog for a few seconds while she is sitting, then tell her to go play again. For especially fast recalls, offer a couple of training treats and take the time to praise and pet the dog enthusiastically before releasing her. The dog will learn that coming when called is not necessarily the end of the play session, and neither is it the end of the world; rather, it signals an enjoyable, quality time-out with the owner before resuming play once more. In fact, playing in the park now becomes a very effective life-reward, which works to facilitate training by reinforcing each obedient and timely recall. Good news!

Sit, Down, Stand and Rollover

Teaching the dog a variety of body positions is easy for owner and dog, impressive for spectators and extremely useful for all. Using lure-reward techniques, it is possible to train several positions at once to verbal commands or hand signals (which impress the socks off onlookers).

Sit and **down**—the two control commands—prevent or resolve nearly a hundred behavior problems. For example, if the dog happily and obediently sits or lies down when requested, she cannot jump on visitors, dash out the front door, run around and chase her tail, pester other dogs, harass cats or annoy family, friends or strangers. Additionally, "Sit" or "Down" are the best emergency commands for off-leash control.

It is easier to teach and maintain a reliable sit than maintain a reliable recall. *Sit* is the purest and simplest of commands—either the dog is sitting or she is not. If there is any change of circumstances or potential danger in the park, for example, simply instruct the dog to sit. If she sits, you have a number of options: Allow the dog to resume playing when she is safe, walk up and put the dog on leash or call the dog. The dog will be much more likely to come when called if she has already acknowledged her compliance by sitting. If the dog does not sit in the park—train her to!

Stand and **rollover-stay** are the two positions for examining the dog. Your veterinarian will love you to distraction if you take a little time to teach the dog to stand still and roll over and play possum. Also, your vet bills will be smaller because it will take the veterinarian less time to examine your dog. The rollover-stay is an especially useful command and is really just a variation of the down-stay: Whereas the dog lies prone in the traditional down, she lies supine in the rollover-stay.

As with teaching come and sit, the training techniques to teach the dog to assume all other body positions on cue are user-friendly and dog-friendly. Simply give the appropriate request, lure the dog into the desired body position using a training treat or toy and then *praise* (and maybe reward) the dog as soon as she complies. Try not to touch the dog to get her to respond. If you teach the dog by guiding her into position, the dog will quickly learn that rump-pressure means sit, for example, but as yet you still have no control over your dog if she is just 6 feet away. It will still be necessary to teach the dog to sit on request. So do not make training a time-consuming two-step process; instead, teach the dog to sit to a verbal request or hand signal from the outset. Once the dog sits willingly when requested, by all means use your hands to pet the dog when she does so.

To teach *down* when the dog is already sitting, say "Tina, down!," hold the lure in one hand (palm down) and lower that hand to the floor between the dog's forepaws. As the dog lowers her head to follow the lure, slowly move the lure away from the dog just a fraction (in front of her paws). The dog will lie down as she stretches her nose forward to follow the lure. Praise the dog when she does so. If the dog stands up, you pulled the lure away too far and too quickly.

When teaching the dog to lie down from the standing position, say "Down" and lower the lure to the floor as before. Once the dog has lowered her forequarters and assumed a play bow, gently and slowly move the lure *towards* the dog between her forelegs. Praise the dog as soon as her rear end plops down.

After just a couple of trials it will be possible to alternate sits and downs and have the dog energetically perform doggy push-ups. Praise the dog a lot, and after half a dozen or so push-ups reward the dog with a training treat or toy. You will notice the more energetically you move your arm—upwards (palm up) to get the dog to sit, and downwards (palm down) to get the dog to lie down—the more energetically the dog responds to your requests. Now try training the dog in silence and you will notice she has also learned to respond to hand signals. Yeah! Not too shabby for the first session.

To teach *stand* from the sitting position, say "Tina, stand," slowly move the lure half a dog-length away from the dog's nose, keeping it at nose level, and praise the dog as she stands to follow the lure. As soon

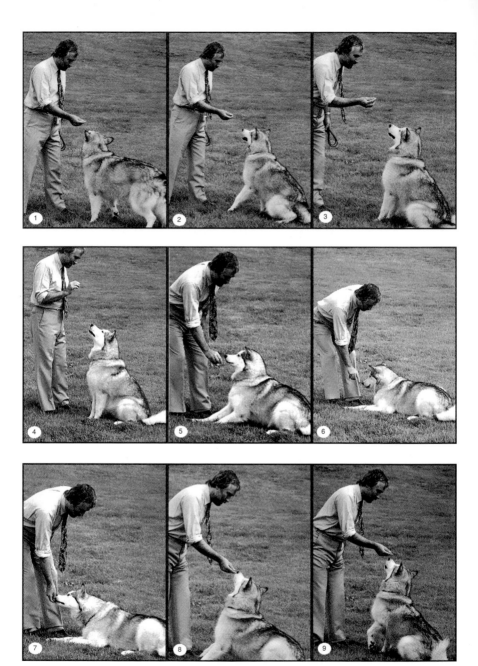

Using a food lure to teach sit, down and stand. 1) "Phoenix, sit." 2) Hand palm upwards, move lure up and back over dog's muzzle. 3) "Good sit, Phoenix!" 4) "Phoenix, down." 5) Hand palm downwards, move lure down to lie between dog's forepaws. 6) "Phoenix, off. Good down, Phoenix!" 7) "Phoenix, sit!" 8) Palm upwards, move lure up and back, keeping it close to dog's muzzle. 9) "Good sit, Phoenix!"

10) *"Phoenix, stand!"* 11) *Move lure away from dog at nose height, then lower it a tad.* 12) *"Phoenix, off! Good stand, Phoenix!"* 13) *"Phoenix, down!"* 14) *Hand palm downwards, move lure down to lie between dog's forepaws.* 15) *"Phoenix, off! Good down-stay, Phoenix!"* 16) *"Phoenix, stand!"* 17) *Move lure away from dog's muzzle up to nose height.* 18) *"Phoenix, off! Good stand-stay, Phoenix. Now we'll make the vet and groomer happy!"*

as the dog stands, lower the lure to just beneath the dog's chin to entice her to look down; otherwise she will stand and then sit immediately. To prompt the dog to stand from the down position, move the lure half a dog-length upwards and away from the dog, holding the lure at standing nose height from the floor.

Teaching **rollover** is best started from the down position, with the dog lying on one side, or at least with both hind legs stretched out on the same side. Say "Tina, bang!" and move the lure backwards and alongside the dog's muzzle to her elbow (on the side of her outstretched hind legs). Once the dog looks to the side and backwards, very slowly move the lure upwards to the dog's shoulder and backbone. Tickling the dog in the goolies (groin area) often invokes a reflex-raising of the hind leg as an appeasement gesture, which facilitates the tendency to roll over. If you move the lure too quickly and the dog jumps into the standing position, have patience and start again. As soon as the dog rolls onto her back, keep the lure stationary and mesmerize the dog with a relaxing tummy rub.

To teach **rollover-stay** when the dog is standing or moving, say "Tina, bang!" and give the appropriate hand signal (with index finger pointed and thumb cocked in true Sam Spade fashion), then in one fluid movement lure her to first lie down and then rollover-stay as above.

Teaching the dog to **stay** in each of the above four positions becomes a piece of cake after first teaching the dog not to worry at the toy or treat training lure. This is best accomplished by hand feeding dinner kibble. Hold a piece of kibble firmly in your hand and softly instruct "Off!" Ignore any licking and slobbering *for however long the dog worries at the treat,* but say "Take it!" and offer the kibble *the instant* the dog breaks contact with her muzzle. Repeat this a few times, and then up the ante and insist the dog remove her muzzle for one whole second before offering the kibble. Then progressively refine your criteria and have the dog not touch your hand (or treat) for longer and longer periods on each trial, such as for two seconds, four seconds, then six, ten, fifteen, twenty, thirty seconds and so on.

The dog soon learns: (1) worrying at the treat never gets results, whereas (2) noncontact is often rewarded after a variable time lapse.

Teaching *"Off!"* has many useful applications in its own right. Additionally, instructing the dog not to touch a training lure often produces spontaneous and magical stays. Request the dog to stand-stay, for example, and not to touch the lure. At first set your sights on a short two-second stay before rewarding the dog. (Remember, every long journey begins with a single step.) However, on subsequent trials, gradually and progressively increase the length of stay required to receive a reward. In no time at all your dog will stand calmly for a minute or so.

Relevancy Training

Once you have taught the dog what you expect her to do when requested to come, sit, lie down, stand, rollover and stay, the time is right to teach the dog *why* she should comply with your wishes. The secret is to have many (*many*) extremely short training interludes (two to five seconds each) at numerous (*numerous*) times during the course of the dog's day. Especially work with the dog immediately *before* the dog's good times and *during* the dog's good times. For example, ask your dog to sit and/or lie down each time before opening doors, serving meals, offering treats and tummy rubs; ask the dog to perform a few controlled doggy push-ups before letting her off leash or throwing a tennis ball; and perhaps request the dog to sit-down-sit-stand-down-stand-rollover before inviting her to cuddle on the couch.

Similarly, request the dog to sit many times during play or on walks, and in no time at all the dog will be only too pleased to follow your instructions because she has learned that a compliant response heralds all sorts of goodies. Basically all you are trying to teach the dog is how to say please: "Please throw the tennis ball. Please may I snuggle on the couch."

Remember, it is important to keep training interludes short and to have many short sessions each and every day. The shortest (and most useful) session comprises asking the dog to sit and then go play during a play session. When trained this way, your dog will soon associate training with good times. In fact, the dog may be unable to distinguish between training and good times and, indeed, there should be no distinction. The warped concept that training involves forcing the dog to comply and/or dominating her will is totally at odds with the picture of a truly well-trained dog. In reality, enjoying a game of training with a dog is no different from enjoying a game of backgammon or tennis with a friend; and walking with a dog should be no different from strolling with a spouse, or with buddies on the golf course.

Walk by Your Side

Many people attempt to teach a dog to heel by putting her on a leash and physically correcting the dog when she makes mistakes. There are a number of things seriously wrong with this approach, the first being that most people do not want precision heeling; rather, they simply want the dog to follow or walk by their side. Second, when physically restrained during "training," even though the dog may grudgingly mope by your side when "handcuffed" on leash, let's see what happens when she is off leash. History! The dog is in the next county because she never enjoyed walking with you on leash and you have no control over her off leash. So let's just teach the dog off leash from the outset to *want* to walk with us. Third, if the dog has not been trained to heel, it is a trifle hasty to think about punishing the poor dog for making mistakes and breaking heeling rules she didn't even know existed. This is simply not fair! Surely, if the dog had been adequately taught how to heel, she would seldom make mistakes and hence there would be no need to correct the dog. Remember, each mistake and each correction (punishment) advertise the trainer's inadequacy, not the dog's. The dog is not stubborn, she is not stupid and she is not bad. Even if she were, she would still require training, so let's train her properly.

Let's teach the dog to *enjoy* following us and to *want* to walk by our side off leash. Then it will be easier to teach high-precision off-leash heeling patterns if desired. Before going on outdoor walks, it is necessary to teach the dog not to pull. Then it becomes easy to teach on-leash walking and heeling because the dog already wants to walk with you, she is familiar with the desired walking and heeling positions and she knows not to pull.

FOLLOWING

Start by training your dog to follow you. Many puppies will follow if you simply walk away from them and maybe click your fingers or chuckle. Adult dogs may require additional enticement to stimulate them to follow, such as a training lure or, at the very least, a lively trainer. To teach the dog to follow: (1) keep walking and (2) walk away from the dog. If the dog attempts to lead or lag, change pace; slow down if the dog forges too far ahead, but speed up if she lags too far behind. Say "Steady!" or "Easy!" each time before you slow down and "Quickly!" or "Hustle!" each time before you speed up, and the dog will learn to change pace on cue. If the dog lags or leads too far, or if she wanders right or left, simply walk quickly in the opposite direction and maybe even run away from the dog and hide.

Practicing is a lot of fun; you can set up a course in your home, yard or park to do this. Indoors, entice the dog to follow upstairs, into a bedroom, into the bathroom, downstairs, around the living room couch, zigzagging between dining room chairs and into the kitchen for dinner. Outdoors, get the dog to follow around park benches, trees, shrubs and along walkways and lines in the grass. (For safety outdoors, it is advisable to attach a long line on the dog, but never exert corrective tension on the line.)

Remember, following has a lot to do with attitude—
your attitude! Most probably your dog will *not* want to
follow Mr. Grumpy Troll with the personality of wilted
lettuce. Lighten up—walk with a jaunty step, whistle a
happy tune, sing, skip and tell jokes to your dog and
she will be right there by your side.

BY YOUR SIDE

It is smart to train the dog to walk close on one side or
the other—either side will do, your choice. When walking, jogging or cycling, it is generally bad news to have
the dog suddenly cut in front of you. In fact, I train my
dogs to walk "By my side" and "Other side"—both very
useful instructions. It is possible to position the dog
fairly accurately by looking to the appropriate side and
clicking your fingers or slapping your thigh on that
side. A precise positioning may be attained by holding
a training lure, such as a chew toy, tennis ball or food
treat. Stop and stand still several times throughout the
walk, just as you would when window shopping or
meeting a friend. Use the lure to make sure the dog
slows down and stays close whenever you stop.

When teaching the dog to heel, we generally want
her to sit in heel position when we stop. Teach heel

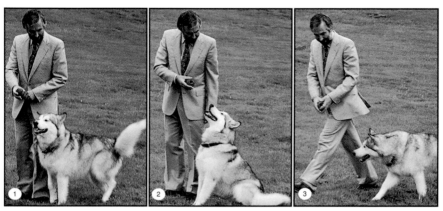

Using a toy to teach sit-heel-sit sequences: 1) "Phoenix, sit!" Standing still, move lure up and back over dog's muzzle . . . 2) to position dog sitting in heel position on your left side. 3) Say "Phoenix, heel!" and walk ahead, wagging lure in left hand. Change lure to right hand in preparation for sit signal. Say "Sit" and then . . .

position at the standstill and the dog will learn that the default heel position is sitting by your side (left or right—your choice, unless you wish to compete in obedience trials, in which case the dog must heel on the left).

Several times a day, stand up and call your dog to come and sit in heel position—"Tina, heel!" For example, instruct the dog to come to heel each time there are commercials on TV, or each time you turn a page of a novel, and the dog will get it in a single evening.

Practice straight-line heeling and turns separately. With the dog sitting at heel, teach her to turn in place. After each quarter-turn, half-turn or full turn in place, lure the dog to sit at heel. Now it's time for short straight-line heeling sequences, no more than a few steps at a time. Always think of heeling in terms of sit-heel-sit sequences—start and end with the dog in position and do your best to keep her there when moving. Progressively increase the number of steps in each sequence. When the dog remains close for 20 yards of straight-line heeling, it is time to add a few turns and then sign up for a happy-heeling obedience class to get some advice from the experts,

4) use hand signal to lure dog to sit as you stop. Eventually, dog will sit automatically at heel whenever you stop. 5) "Good dog!"

No Pulling on Leash

You can start teaching your dog not to pull on leash anywhere—in front of the television or outdoors—but regardless of location, you must not take a single step with tension in the leash. For a reason known only to dogs, even just a couple of paces of pulling on leash is intrinsically motivating and diabolically rewarding. Instead, attach the leash to the dog's collar, grasp the other end firmly with both hands held close to your chest, and stand still—do not budge an inch. Have somebody watch you with a stopwatch to time your progress, or else you will never believe this will work and so you will not even try the exercise, and your shoulder and the dog's neck will be traumatized for years to come.

Stand still and wait for the dog to stop pulling, and to sit and/or lie down. All dogs stop pulling and sit eventually. Most take only a couple of minutes; the all-time record is 22½ minutes. Time how long it takes. Gently praise the dog when she stops pulling, and as soon as she sits, enthusiastically praise the dog and take just one step forward, then immediately stand still. This single step usually demonstrates the ballistic reinforcing nature of pulling on leash; most dogs explode to the end of the leash, so be prepared for the strain. Stand firm and wait for the dog to sit again. Repeat this half a dozen times and you will probably notice a progressive reduction in the force of the dog's one-step explosions and a radical reduction in the time it takes for the dog to sit each time.

As the dog learns "Sit we go" and "Pull we stop," she will begin to walk forward calmly with each single step and automatically sit when you stop. Now try two steps before you stop. Wooooooo! Scary! When the dog has mastered two steps at a time, try for three. After each success, progressively increase the number of steps in the sequence: try four steps and then six, eight, ten and twenty steps before stopping. Congratulations! You are now walking the dog on leash.

Whenever walking with the dog (off leash or on leash), make sure you stop periodically to practice a few position commands and stays before instructing the dog to "Walk on!" (Remember, you want the dog to be compliant everywhere, not just in the kitchen when her dinner is at hand.) For example, stopping every 25 yards to briefly train the dog amounts to over 200 training interludes within a single 3-mile stroll. And each training session is in a different location. You will not believe the improvement within just the first mile of the first walk.

To put it another way, integrating training into a walk offers 200 separate opportunities to use the continuance of the walk as a reward to reinforce the dog's education. Moreover, some training interludes may comprise continuing education for the dog's walking skills: Alternate short periods of the dog walking calmly by your side with periods when the dog is allowed to sniff and investigate the environment. Now sniffing odors on the grass and meeting other dogs become rewards which reinforce the dog's calm and mannerly demeanor. Good Lord! Whatever next? Many enjoyable walks together of course. Happy trails!

THE IMPORTANCE OF TRICKS

Nothing will improve a dog's quality of life better than having a few tricks under her belt. Teaching any trick expands the dog's vocabulary, which facilitates communication and improves the owner's control. Also, specific tricks help prevent and resolve specific behavior problems. For example, by teaching the dog to fetch her toys, the dog learns carrying a toy makes the owner happy and, therefore, will be more likely to chew her toy than other inappropriate items.

More important, teaching tricks prompts owners to lighten up and train with a sunny disposition. Really, tricks should be no different from any other behaviors we put on cue. But they are. When teaching tricks, owners have a much sweeter attitude, which in turn motivates the dog and improves her willingness to comply. The dog feels tricks are a blast, but formal commands are a drag. In fact, tricks are so enjoyable, they may be used as rewards in training by asking the dog to come, sit and down-stay and then rollover for a tummy rub. Go on, try it: Crack a smile and even giggle when the dog promptly and willingly lies down and stays.

Most important, performing tricks prompts onlookers to smile and giggle. Many people are scared of dogs, especially large ones. And nothing can be more off-putting for a dog than to be constantly confronted by strangers who don't like her because of her size or the way she looks. Uneasy people put the dog on edge, causing her to back off and bark, only frightening people all the more. And so a vicious circle develops, with the people's fear fueling the dog's fear *and vice versa*. Instead, tie a pink ribbon to your dog's collar and practice all sorts of tricks on walks and in the park, and you will be pleasantly amazed how it changes people's attitudes toward your friendly dog. The dog's repertoire of tricks is limited only by the trainer's imagination. Below I have described three of my favorites:

SPEAK AND SHUSH

The training sequence involved in teaching a dog to bark on request is no different from that used when training any behavior on cue: request—lure—response—reward. As always, the secret of success lies in finding an effective lure. If the dog always barks at the doorbell, for example, say "Rover, speak!", have an accomplice ring the doorbell, then reward the dog for barking. After a few woofs, ask Rover to "Shush!", waggle a food treat under her nose (to entice her to sniff and thus to shush), praise her when quiet and eventually offer the treat as a reward. Alternate "Speak" and "Shush," progressively increasing the length of shush-time between each barking bout.

PLAY BOW

With the dog standing, say "Bow!" and lower the food lure (palm upwards) to rest between the dog's forepaws. Praise as the dog lowers

her forequarters and sternum to the ground (as when teaching the down), but then lure the dog to stand and offer the treat. On successive trials, gradually increase the length of time the dog is required to remain in the play bow posture in order to gain a food reward. If the dog's rear end collapses into a down, say nothing and offer no reward; simply start over.

BE A BEAR

With the dog sitting backed into a corner to prevent her from toppling over backwards, say "Be a bear!" With bent paw and palm down, raise a lure upwards and backwards along the top of the dog's muzzle. Praise the dog when she sits up on her haunches and offer the treat as a reward. To prevent the dog from standing on her hind legs, keep the lure closer to the dog's muzzle. On each trial, progressively increase the length of time the dog is required to sit up to receive a food reward. Since lure-reward training is so easy, teach the dog to stand and walk on her hind legs as well!

Teaching "Be a Bear"

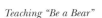

chapter 9

Getting
Active
with your Dog

by Bardi McLennan

Once you and your dog have graduated from basic obedience training and are beginning to work together as a team, you can take part in the growing world of dog activities. There are so many fun things to do with your dog! Just remember, people and dogs don't always learn at the same pace, so don't be upset if you (or your dog) need more than two basic training courses before your team becomes operational. Even smart dogs don't go straight to college from kindergarten!

Just as there are events geared to certain types of dogs, so there are ones that are more appealing to certain types of people. In some

128

activities, you give the commands and your dog does the work (upland game hunting is one example), while in others, such as agility, you'll both get a workout. You may want to aim for prestigious titles to add to your dog's name, or you may want nothing more than the sheer enjoyment of being around other people and their dogs. Passive or active, participation has its own rewards.

Consider your dog's physical capabilities when looking into any of the canine activities. It's easy to see that a Basset Hound is not built for the racetrack, nor would a Chihuahua be the breed of choice for pulling a sled. A loyal dog will attempt almost anything you ask him to do, so it is up to you to know your dog's limitations. A dog must be physically sound in order to compete at any level in athletic activities, and being mentally sound is a definite plus. Advanced age, however, may not be a deterrent. Many dogs still hunt and herd at ten or twelve years of age. It's entirely possible for dogs to be "fit at 50." Take your dog for a checkup, explain to your vet the type of activity you have in mind and be guided by his or her findings.

*All dogs seem
to love playing
flyball.*

You needn't be restricted to breed-specific sports if it's only fun you're after. Certain AKC activities are limited to designated breeds; however, as each new trial, test or sport has grown in popularity, so has the variety of breeds encouraged to participate at a fun level.

But don't shortchange your fun, or that of your dog, by thinking only of the basic function of her breed. Once a dog has learned how to learn, she can be taught to do just about anything as long as the size of the dog is right for the job and you both think it is fun and rewarding. In other words, you are a team.

To get involved in any of the activities detailed in this chapter, look for the names and addresses of the organizations that sponsor them in Chapter 13. You can also ask your breeder or a local dog trainer for contacts.

You can compete in obedience trials with a well trained dog.

Official American Kennel Club Activities

The following tests and trials are some of the events sanctioned by the AKC and sponsored by various dog clubs. Your dog's expertise will be rewarded with impressive titles. You can participate just for fun, or be competitive and go for those awards.

OBEDIENCE

Training classes begin with pups as young as three months of age in kindergarten puppy training, then advance to pre-novice (all exercises on lead) and go on to novice, which is where you'll start off-lead work. In obedience classes dogs learn to sit, stay, heel and come through a variety of exercises. Once you've got the basics down, you can enter obedience trials and work toward earning your dog's first degree, a C.D. (Companion Dog).

The next level is called "Open," in which jumps and retrieves perk up the dog's interest. Passing grades in competition at this level earn a C.D.X. (Companion Dog Excellent). Beyond that lies the goal of the most ambitious—Utility (U.D. and even U.D.X. or OTCh, an Obedience Champion).

AGILITY

All dogs can participate in the latest canine sport to have gained worldwide popularity for its fun and excitement, agility. It began in England as a canine version of horse show-jumping, but because dogs are more agile and able to perform on verbal commands, extra feats were added such as climbing, balancing and racing through tunnels or in and out of weave poles. Many of the obstacles (regulation or homemade) can be set up in your own backyard. If the agility bug bites, you could end up in international competition!

For starters, your dog should be obedience trained, even though, in the beginning, the lessons may all be taught on lead. Once the dog understands the commands (and you do, too), it's as easy as guiding the dog over a prescribed course, one obstacle at a time. In competition, the race is against the clock, so wear your running shoes! The dog starts with 200 points and the judge deducts for infractions and misadventures along the way.

All dogs seem to love agility and respond to it as if they were being turned loose in a playground paradise. Your dog's enthusiasm will be contagious; agility turns into great fun for dog and owner.

FIELD TRIALS AND HUNTING TESTS

There are field trials and hunting tests for the sporting breeds—retrievers, spaniels and pointing breeds, and for some hounds—Bassets, Beagles and Dachshunds. Field trials are competitive events that test a dog's ability to perform the functions for which she was bred. Hunting tests, which are open to retrievers,

---

TITLES AWARDED BY THE AKC

Conformation: Ch. (Champion)

Obedience: CD (Companion Dog); CDX (Companion Dog Excellent); UD (Utility Dog); UDX (Utility Dog Excellent); OTCh. (Obedience Trial Champion)

Field: JH (Junior Hunter); SH (Senior Hunter); MH (Master Hunter); AFCh. (Amateur Field Champion); FCh. (Field Champion)

Lure Coursing: JC (Junior Courser); SC (Senior Courser)

Herding: HT (Herding Tested); PT (Pre-Trial Tested); HS (Herding Started); HI (Herding Intermediate); HX (Herding Excellent); HCh. (Herding Champion)

Tracking: TD (Tracking Dog); TDX (Tracking Dog Excellent)

Agility: NAD (Novice Agility); OAD (Open Agility); ADX (Agility Excellent); MAX (Master Agility)

Earthdog Tests: JE (Junior Earthdog); SE (Senior Earthdog); ME (Master Earthdog)

Canine Good Citizen: CGC

Combination: DC (Dual Champion—Ch. and Fch.); TC (Triple Champion—Ch., Fch., and OTCh.)

spaniels and pointing breeds only, are noncompetitive and are a means of judging the dog's ability as well as that of the handler.

Hunting is a very large and complex part of canine sports, and if you own one of the breeds that hunts, the events are a great treat for your dog and you. He gets to do what he was bred for, and you get to work with him and watch him do it. You'll be proud of and amazed at what your dog can do.

Retrievers and other sporting breeds get to do what they're bred to in hunting tests.

Fortunately, the AKC publishes a series of booklets on these events, which outline the rules and regulations and include a glossary of the sometimes complicated terms. The AKC also publishes newsletters for field trialers and hunting test enthusiasts. The United Kennel Club (UKC) also has informative materials for the hunter and his dog.

HERDING TESTS AND TRIALS

Herding, like hunting, dates back to the first known uses man made of dogs. The interest in herding today is widespread, and if you own a herding breed, you can join in the activity. Herding dogs are tested for their natural skills to keep a flock of ducks, sheep or cattle together. If your dog shows potential, you can start at the testing level, where your dog can earn a title for showing an inherent herding ability. With training you can advance to the trial level, where your dog should be capable of controlling even difficult livestock in diverse situations.

LURE COURSING

The AKC Tests and Trials for Lure Coursing are open to traditional sighthounds—Greyhounds, Whippets,

Borzoi, Salukis, Afghan Hounds, Ibizan Hounds and Scottish Deerhounds—as well as to Basenjis and Rhodesian Ridgebacks. Hounds are judged on overall ability, follow, speed, agility and endurance. This is possibly the most exciting of the trials for spectators, because the speed and agility of the dogs is awesome to watch as they chase the lure (or "course") in heats of two or three dogs at a time.

TRACKING

Tracking is another activity in which almost any dog can compete because every dog that sniffs the ground when taken outdoors is, in fact, tracking. The hard part comes when the rules as to what, when and where the dog tracks are determined by a person, not the dog! Tracking tests cover a large area of fields, woods and roads. The tracks are laid hours before the dogs go to work on them, and include "tricks" like cross-tracks and sharp turns. If you're interested in search-and-rescue work, this is the place to start.

This tracking dog is hot on the trail.

EARTHDOG TESTS FOR SMALL TERRIERS AND DACHSHUNDS

These tests are open to Australian, Bedlington, Border, Cairn, Dandie Dinmont, Smooth and Wire Fox, Lakeland, Norfolk, Norwich, Scottish, Sealyham, Skye, Welsh and West Highland White Terriers as well as Dachshunds. The dogs need no prior training for this terrier sport. There is a qualifying test on the day of the event, so dog and handler learn the rules on the spot. These tests, or "digs," sometimes end with informal races in the late afternoon.

133

Enjoying Your
Dog

Here are some of the extracurricular obedience and racing activities that are not regulated by the AKC or UKC, but are generally run by clubs or a group of dog fanciers and are often open to all.

Canine Freestyle This activity is something new on the scene and is variously likened to dancing, dressage or ice skating. It is meant to show the athleticism of the dog, but also requires showmanship on the part of the dog's handler. If you and your dog like to ham it up for friends, you might want to look into freestyle.

Lure coursing lets sighthounds do what they do best—run!

Scent Hurdle Racing Scent hurdle racing is purely a fun activity sponsored by obedience clubs with members forming competing teams. The height of the hurdles is based on the size of the shortest dog on the team. On a signal, one team dog is released on each of two side-by-side courses and must clear every hurdle before picking up its own dumbbell from a platform and returning over the jumps to the handler. As each dog returns, the next on that team is sent. Of course, that is what the dogs are supposed to do. When the dogs improvise (going under or around the hurdles, stealing another dog's dumbbell, and so forth), it no doubt frustrates the handlers, but just adds to the fun for everyone else.

Flyball This type of racing is similar, but after negotiating the four hurdles, the dog comes to a flyball box, steps on a lever that releases a tennis ball into the air, catches the ball and returns over the hurdles to the starting point. This game also becomes extremely fun for spectators because the dogs sometimes cheat by catching a ball released by the dog in the next lane. Three titles can be earned—Flyball Dog (F.D.), Flyball Dog Excellent (F.D.X.) and Flyball Dog Champion (Fb.D.Ch.)—all awarded by the North American Flyball Association, Inc.

Dogsledding The name conjures up the Rocky Mountains or the frigid North, but you can find dogsled clubs in such unlikely spots as Maryland, North Carolina and Virginia! Dogsledding is primarily for the Nordic breeds such as the Alaskan Malamutes, Siberian Huskies and Samoyeds, but other breeds can try. There are some practical backyard applications to this sport, too. With parental supervision, almost any strong dog could pull a child's sled.

Coming over the A-frame on an agility course.

These are just some of the many recreational ways you can get to know and understand your multifaceted dog better and have fun doing it.

chapter 10

Your Dog
and your
Family

by Bardi McLennan

Adding a dog automatically increases your family by one, no matter whether you live alone in an apartment or are part of a mother, father and six kids household. The single-person family is fair game for numerous and varied canine misconceptions as to who is dog and who pays the bills, whereas a dog in a houseful of children will consider himself to be just one of the gang, littermates all. One dog and one child may give a dog reason to believe they are both kids or both dogs.

Either interpretation requires parental supervision and sometimes speedy intervention.

As soon as one paw goes through the door into your home, Rufus (or Rufina) has to make many adjustments to become a part of your family. Your job is to make him fit in as painlessly as possible. An older dog may have some frame of reference from past experience, but to a 10-week-old puppy, everything is brand new: people, furniture, stairs, when and where people eat, sleep or watch TV, his own place and everyone else's space, smells, sounds, outdoors—everything!

Puppies, and newly acquired dogs of any age, do not need what we think of as "freedom." If you leave a new dog or puppy loose in the house, you will almost certainly return to chaotic destruction and the dog will forever after equate your homecoming with a time of punishment to be dreaded. It is unfair to give your dog what amounts to "freedom to get into trouble." Instead, confine him to a crate for brief periods of your absence (up to three or four hours) and, for the long haul, a workday for example, confine him to one untrashable area with his own toys, a bowl of water and a radio left on (low) in another room.

Lots of pets get along with each other just fine.

For the first few days, when not confined, put Rufus on a long leash tied to your wrist or waist. This umbilical cord method enables the dog to learn all about you from your body language and voice, and to learn by his own actions which things in the house are NO! and which ones are rewarded by "Good dog." Housetraining will be easier with the pup always by your side. Speaking of which, accidents do happen. That goal of "completely housetrained" takes up to a year, or the length of time it takes the pup to mature.

The All-Adult Family

Most dogs in an adults-only household today are likely to be latchkey pets, with no one home all day but the dog. When you return after a tough day on the job, the dog can and should be your relaxation therapy. But going home can instead be a daily frustration.

Separation anxiety is a very common problem for the dog in a working household. It may begin with whines and barks of loneliness, but it will soon escalate into a frenzied destruction derby. That is why it is so important to set aside the time to teach a dog to relax when left alone in his confined area and to understand that he can trust you to return.

Let the dog get used to your work schedule in easy stages. Confine him to one room and go in and out of that room over and over again. Be casual about it. No physical, voice or eye contact. When the pup no longer even notices your comings and goings, leave the house for varying lengths of time, returning to stay home for a few minutes and gradually increasing the time away. This training can take days, but the dog is learning that you haven't left him forever and that he can trust you.

Any time you leave the dog, but especially during this training period, be casual about your departure. No anxiety-building fond farewells. Just "Bye" and go! Remember the "Good dog" when you return to find everything more or less as you left it.

If things are a mess (or even a disaster) when you return, greet the dog, take him outside to eliminate, and then put him in his crate while you clean up. Rant and rave in the shower! *Do not* punish the dog. You were not there when it happened, and the rule is: Only punish as you catch the dog in the act of wrongdoing. Obviously, it makes sense to get your latchkey puppy when you'll have a week or two to spend on these training essentials.

Family weekend activities should include Rufus whenever possible. Depending on the pup's age, now is the time for a long walk in the park, playtime in the backyard, a hike in the woods. Socializing is as important as health care, good food and physical exercise, so visiting Aunt Emma or Uncle Harry and the next-door neighbor's dog or cat is essential to developing an outgoing, friendly temperament in your pet.

If you are a single adult, socializing Rufus at home and away will prevent him from becoming overly protective of you (or just overly attached) and will also prevent such behavioral problems as dominance or fear of strangers.

Babies

Whether already here or on the way, babies figure larger than life in the eyes of a dog. If the dog is there first, let him in on all your baby preparations in the house. When baby arrives, let Rufus sniff any item of clothing that has been on the baby before Junior comes home. Then let Mom greet the dog first before introducing the new family member. Hold the baby down for the dog to see and sniff, but make sure someone's holding the dog on lead in case of any sudden moves. Don't play keepaway or tease the dog with the baby, which only invites undesirable jumping up.

The dog and the baby are "family," and for starters can be treated almost as equals. Things rapidly change, however, especially when baby takes to creeping around on all fours on the dog's turf or, better yet, has yummy pudding all over her face and hands! That's when a lot of things in the dog's and baby's lives become more separate than equal.

Dogs are perfect confidants.

Toddlers make terrible dog owners, but if you can't avoid the combination, use patient discipline (that is, positive teaching rather than punishment), and use time-outs before you run out of patience.

Enjoying Your
Dog

A dog and a baby (or toddler, or an assertive young child) should never be left alone together. Take the dog with you or confine him. With a baby or youngsters in the house, you'll have plenty of use for that wonderful canine safety device called a crate!

Young Children

Any dog in a house with kids will behave pretty much as the kids do, good or bad. But even good dogs and good children can get into trouble when play becomes rowdy and active.

Teach children how to play nicely with a puppy.

Legs bobbing up and down, shrill voices screeching, a ball hurtling overhead, all add up to exuberant frustration for a dog who's just trying to be part of the gang. In a pack of puppies, any legs or toys being chased would be caught by a set of teeth, and all the pups involved would understand that is how the game is played. Kids do not understand this, nor do parents tolerate it. Bring Rufus indoors before you have reason to regret it. This is time-out, not a punishment.

You can explain the situation to the children and tell them they must play quieter games until the puppy learns not to grab them with his mouth. Unfortunately, you can't explain it that easily to the dog. With adult supervision, they will learn how to play together.

Young children love to tease. Sticking their faces or wiggling their hands or fingers in the dog's face is teasing. To another person it might be just annoying, but it is threatening to a dog. There's another difference: We can make the child stop by an explanation, but the only way a dog can stop it is with a warning growl and then with teeth. Teasing is the major cause of children being bitten by their pets. Treat it seriously.

Older Children

The best age for a child to get a first dog is between the ages of 8 and 12. That's when kids are able to accept some real responsibility for their pet. Even so, take the child's vow of "I will never *ever* forget to feed (brush, walk, etc.) the dog" for what it's worth: a child's good intention at that moment. Most kids today have extra lessons, soccer practice, Little League, ballet, and so forth piled on top of school schedules. There will be many times when Mom will have to come to the dog's rescue. "I walked the dog for you so you can set the table for me" is one way to get around a missed appointment without laying on blame or guilt.

Kids in this age group make excellent obedience trainers because they are into the teaching/learning process themselves and they lack the self-consciousness of adults. Attending a dog show is something the whole family can enjoy, and watching Junior Showmanship may catch the eye of the kids. Older children can begin to get involved in many of the recreational activities that were reviewed in the previous chapter. Some of the agility obstacles, for example, can be set up in the backyard as a family project (with an adult making sure all the equipment is safe and secure for the dog).

Older kids are also beginning to look to the future, and may envision themselves as veterinarians or trainers or show dog handlers or writers of the next Lassie best-seller. Dogs are perfect confidants for these dreams. They won't tell a soul.

Other Pets

Introduce all pets tactfully. In a dog/cat situation, hold the dog, not the cat. Let two dogs meet on neutral turf—a stroll in the park or a walk down the street—with both on loose leads to permit all the normal canine ways of saying hello, including routine sniffing, circling, more sniffing, and so on. Small creatures such as hamsters, chinchillas or mice must be kept safe from their natural predators (dogs and cats).

Festive Family Occasions

Parties are great for people, but not necessarily for puppies. Until all the guests have arrived, put the dog in his crate or in a room where he won't be disturbed. A socialized dog can join the fun later as long as he's not underfoot, annoying guests or into the hors d'oeuvres.

There are a few dangers to consider, too. Doors opening and closing can allow a puppy to slip out unnoticed in the confusion, and you'll be organizing a search party instead of playing host or hostess. Party food and buffet service are not for dogs. Let Rufus party in his crate with a nice big dog biscuit.

At Christmas time, not only are tree decorations dangerous and breakable (and perhaps family heirlooms), but extreme caution should be taken with the lights, cords and outlets for the tree lights and any other festive lighting. Occasionally a dog lifts a leg, ignoring the fact that the tree is indoors. To avoid this, use a canine repellent, made for gardens, on the tree. Or keep him out of the tree room unless supervised. And whatever you do, *don't* invite trouble by hanging his toys on the tree!

Car Travel

Before you plan a vacation by car or RV with Rufus, be sure he enjoys car travel. Nothing spoils a holiday quicker than a carsick dog! Work within the dog's comfort level. Get in the car with the dog in his crate or attached to a canine car safety belt and just sit there until he relaxes. That's all. Next time, get in the car, turn on the engine and go nowhere. Just sit. When that is okay, turn on the engine and go around the block. Now you can go for a ride and include a stop where you get out, leaving the dog for a minute or two.

On a warm day, always park in the shade and leave windows open several inches. And return quickly. It only takes 10 minutes for a car to become an overheated steel death trap.

Motel or Pet Motel?

Not all motels or hotels accept pets, but you have a much better choice today than even a few years ago. To find a dog-friendly lodging, look at *On the Road Again With Man's Best Friend*, a series of directories that detail bed and breakfasts, inns, family resorts and other hotels/motels. Some places require a refundable deposit to cover any damage incurred by the dog. More B&Bs accept pets now, but some restrict the size.

If taking Rufus with you is not feasible, check out boarding kennels in your area. Your veterinarian may offer this service, or recommend a kennel or two he or she is familiar with. Go see the facilities for yourself, ask about exercise, diet, housing, and so on. Or, if you'd rather have Rufus stay home, look into bonded petsitters, many of whom will also bring in the mail and water your plants.

chapter 11

Your Dog
and your
Community

by Bardi McLennan

Step outside your home with your dog and you are no longer just family, you are both part of your community. This is when the phrase "responsible pet ownership" takes on serious implications. For starters, it means you pick up after your dog—not just occasionally, but every time your dog eliminates away from home. That means you have joined the Plastic Baggy Brigade! You always have plastic sandwich bags in your pocket and several in the car. It means you teach your kids how to use them, too. If you think this is "yucky," just imagine what the person (a non-doggy person) who inadvertently steps in the mess thinks!

Your responsibility extends to your neighbors: To their ears (no annoying barking); to their property (their garbage, their lawn, their flower beds, their cat—especially their cat); to their kids (on bikes, at play); to their kids' toys and sports equipment.

There are numerous dog-related laws, ranging from simple dog licensing and leash laws to those holding you liable for any physical injury or property damage done by your dog. These laws are in place to protect everyone in the community, including you and your dog. There are town ordinances and state laws which are by no means the same in all towns or all states. Ignorance of the law won't get you off the hook. The time to find out what the laws are where you live is now.

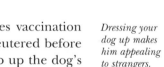

Be sure your dog's license is current. This is not just a good local ordinance, it can make the difference between finding your lost dog or not. Many states now require proof of rabies vaccination and that the dog has been spayed or neutered before issuing a license. At the same time, keep up the dog's annual immunizations.

Dressing your dog up makes him appealing to strangers.

Never let your dog run loose in the neighborhood. This will not only keep you on the right side of the leash law, it's the outdoor version of the rule about not giving your dog "freedom to get into trouble."

Good Canine Citizen

Sometimes it's hard for a dog's owner to assess whether or not the dog is sufficiently socialized to be accepted by the community at large. Does Rufus or Rufina display good, controlled behavior in public? The AKC's Canine Good Citizen program is available through many dog organizations. If your dog passes the test, the title "CGC" is earned.

The overall purpose is to turn your dog into a good neighbor and to teach you about your responsibility to your community as a dog owner. Here are the ten things your dog must do willingly:

1. Accept a stranger stopping to chat with you.
2. Sit and be petted by a stranger.
3. Allow a stranger to handle him or her as a groomer or veterinarian would.
4. Walk nicely on a loose lead.
5. Walk calmly through a crowd.
6. Sit and down on command, then stay in a sit or down position while you walk away.
7. Come when called.
8. Casually greet another dog.
9. React confidently to distractions.
10. Accept being left alone with someone other than you and not become overly agitated or nervous.

Schools and Dogs

Schools are getting involved with pet ownership on an educational level. It has been proven that children who are kind to animals are humane in their attitude toward other people as adults.

A dog is a child's best friend, and so children are often primary pet owners, if not the primary caregivers. Unfortunately, they are also the ones most often bitten by dogs. This occurs due to a lack of understanding that pets, no matter how sweet, cuddly and loving, are still animals. Schools, along with parents, dog clubs, dog fanciers and the AKC, are working to change all that with video programs for children not only in grade school, but in the nursery school and pre-kindergarten age group. Teaching youngsters how to be responsible dog owners is important community work. When your dog has a CGC, volunteer to take part in an educational classroom event put on by your dog club.

Boy Scout Merit Badge

A Merit Badge for Dog Care can be earned by any Boy Scout ages 11 to 18. The requirements are not easy, but amount to a complete course in responsible dog care and general ownership. Here are just a few of the things a Scout must do to earn that badge:

> Point out ten parts of the dog using the correct names.

> Give a report (signed by parent or guardian) on your care of the dog (feeding, food used, housing, exercising, grooming and bathing), plus what has been done to keep the dog healthy.

> Explain the right way to obedience train a dog, and demonstrate three comments.

> Several of the requirements have to do with health care, including first aid, handling a hurt dog, and the dangers of home treatment for a serious ailment.

> The final requirement is to know the local laws and ordinances involving dogs.

There are similar programs for Girl Scouts and 4-H members.

Local Clubs

Local dog clubs are no longer in existence just to put on a yearly dog show. Today, they are apt to be the hub of the community's involvement with pets. Dog clubs conduct educational forums with big-name speakers, stage demonstrations of canine talent in a busy mall and take dogs of various breeds to schools for class-room discussion.

The quickest way to feel accepted as a member in a club is to volunteer your services! Offer to help with something—anything—and watch your popularity (and your interest) grow.

Therapy Dogs

Once your dog has earned that essential CGC and reliably demonstrates a steady, calm temperament, you could look into what therapy dogs are doing in your area.

Therapy dogs go with their owners to visit patients at hospitals or nursing homes, generally remaining on leash but able to coax a pat from a stiffened hand, a smile from a blank face, a few words from sealed lips or a hug from someone in need of love.

Nursing homes cover a wide range of patient care. Some specialize in care of the elderly, some in the treatment of specific illnesses, some in physical therapy. Children's facilities also welcome visits from trained therapy dogs for boosting morale in their pediatric patients. Hospice care for the terminally ill and the at-home care of AIDS patients are other areas where this canine visiting is desperately needed. Therapy dog training comes first.

Your dog can make a differ- ence in lots of lives.

There is a lot more involved than just taking your nice friendly pooch to someone's bedside. Doing therapy dog work involves your own emotional stability as well as that of your dog. But once you have met all the requirements for this work, making the rounds once a week or once a month with your therapy dog is possibly the most rewarding of all community activities.

Disaster Aid

This community service is definitely not for everyone, partly because it is time-consuming. The initial training is rigorous, and there can be no let-up in the continuing workouts, because members are on call 24 hours a day to go wherever they are needed at a moment's notice. But if you think you would like to be able to assist in a disaster, look into search-and-rescue work. The network of search-and-rescue volunteers is worldwide, and all members of the American Rescue Dog Association (ARDA) who are qualified to do this work are volunteers who train and maintain their own dogs.

Physical Aid

Most people are familiar with Seeing Eye dogs, which serve as blind people's eyes, but not with all the other work that dogs are trained to do to assist the disabled. Dogs are also specially trained to pull wheelchairs, carry school books, pick up dropped objects, open and close doors. Some also are ears for the deaf. All these assistance-trained dogs, by the way, are allowed anywhere "No Pet" signs exist (as are therapy dogs when

Making the rounds with your therapy dog can be very rewarding.

properly identified). Getting started in any of this fascinating work requires a background in dog training and canine behavior, but there are also volunteer jobs ranging from answering the phone to cleaning out kennels to providing a foster home for a puppy. You have only to ask.

part four

Beyond
the
Basics

chapter 12

Recommended Reading

Books

ABOUT HEALTH CARE

Ackerman, Lowell. *Guide to Skin and Haircoat Problems in Dogs.* Loveland, Colo.: Alpine Publications, 1994.

Alderton, David. *The Dog Care Manual.* Hauppauge, N.Y.: Barron's Educational Series, Inc., 1986.

American Kennel Club. *American Kennel Club Dog Care and Training.* New York: Howell Book House, 1991.

Bamberger, Michelle, DVM. *Help! The Quick Guide to First Aid for Your Dog.* New York: Howell Book House, 1995.

Carlson, Delbert, DVM, and James Giffin, MD. *Dog Owner's Home Veterinary Handbook.* New York: Howell Book House, 1992.

DeBitetto, James, DVM, and Sarah Hodgson. *You & Your Puppy.* New York: Howell Book House, 1995.

Humphries, Jim, DVM. *Dr. Jim's Animal Clinic for Dogs.* New York: Howell Book House, 1994.

McGinnis, Terri. *The Well Dog Book.* New York: Random House, 1991.

Pitcairn, Richard and Susan. *Natural Health for Dogs.* Emmaus, Pa.: Rodale Press, 1982.

ABOUT DOG SHOWS

Hall, Lynn. *Dog Showing for Beginners.* New York: Howell Book House, 1994.

Nichols, Virginia Tuck. *How to Show Your Own Dog.* Neptune, N. J.: TFH, 1970.

Vanacore, Connie. *Dog Showing, An Owner's Guide.* New York: Howell Book House, 1990.

About Training

Ammen, Amy. *Training in No Time*. New York: Howell Book House, 1995.

Baer, Ted. *Communicating With Your Dog*. Hauppauge, N.Y.: Barron's Educational Series, Inc., 1989.

Benjamin, Carol Lea. *Dog Problems*. New York: Howell Book House, 1989.

Benjamin, Carol Lea. *Dog Training for Kids*. New York: Howell Book House, 1988.

Benjamin, Carol Lea. *Mother Knows Best*. New York: Howell Book House, 1985.

Benjamin, Carol Lea. *Surviving Your Dog's Adolescence*. New York: Howell Book House, 1993.

Bohnenkamp, Gwen. *Manners for the Modern Dog*. San Francisco: Perfect Paws, 1990.

Dibra, Bashkim. *Dog Training by Bash*. New York: Dell, 1992.

Dunbar, Ian, PhD, MRCVS. *Dr. Dunbar's Good Little Dog Book*, James & Kenneth Publishers, 2140 Shattuck Ave. #2406, Berkeley, Calif. 94704. (510) 658–8588. Order from the publisher.

Dunbar, Ian, PhD, MRCVS. *How to Teach a New Dog Old Tricks*, James & Kenneth Publishers. Order from the publisher; address above.

Dunbar, Ian, PhD, MRCVS, and Gwen Bohnenkamp. Booklets on *Preventing Aggression; Housetraining; Chewing; Digging; Barking; Socialization; Fearfulness; and Fighting*, James & Kenneth Publishers. Order from the publisher; address above.

Evans, Job Michael. *People, Pooches and Problems*. New York: Howell Book House, 1991.

Kilcommons, Brian and Sarah Wilson. *Good Owners, Great Dogs*. New York: Warner Books, 1992.

McMains, Joel M. *Dog Logic—Companion Obedience*. New York: Howell Book House, 1992.

Rutherford, Clarice and David H. Neil, MRCVS. *How to Raise a Puppy You Can Live With*. Loveland, Colo.: Alpine Publications, 1982.

Volhard, Jack and Melissa Bartlett. *What All Good Dogs Should Know: The Sensible Way to Train*. New York: Howell Book House, 1991.

About Breeding

Harris, Beth J. Finder. *Breeding a Litter, The Complete Book of Prenatal and Postnatal Care*. New York: Howell Book House, 1983.

Holst, Phyllis, DVM. *Canine Reproduction*. Loveland, Colo.: Alpine Publications, 1985.

Walkowicz, Chris and Bonnie Wilcox, DVM. *Successful Dog Breeding, The Complete Handbook of Canine Midwifery.* New York: Howell Book House, 1994.

ABOUT ACTIVITIES

American Rescue Dog Association. *Search and Rescue Dogs.* New York: Howell Book House, 1991.

Barwig, Susan and Stewart Hilliard. *Schutzhund.* New York: Howell Book House, 1991.

Beaman, Arthur S. *Lure Coursing.* New York: Howell Book House, 1994.

Daniels, Julie. *Enjoying Dog Agility—From Backyard to Competition.* New York: Doral Publishing, 1990.

Davis, Kathy Diamond. *Therapy Dogs.* New York: Howell Book House, 1992.

Gallup, Davis Anne. *Running With Man's Best Friend.* Loveland, Colo.: Alpine Publications, 1986.

Habgood, Dawn and Robert. *On the Road Again With Man's Best Friend.* New England, Mid-Atlantic, West Coast and Southeast editions. Selective guides to area bed and breakfasts, inns, hotels and resorts that welcome guests and their dogs. New York: Howell Book House, 1995.

Holland, Vergil S. *Herding Dogs.* New York: Howell Book House, 1994.

LaBelle, Charlene G. *Backpacking With Your Dog.* Loveland, Colo.: Alpine Publications, 1993.

Simmons-Moake, Jane. *Agility Training, The Fun Sport for All Dogs.* New York: Howell Book House, 1991.

Spencer, James B. *Hup! Training Flushing Spaniels the American Way.* New York: Howell Book House, 1992.

Spencer, James B. *Point! Training the All-Seasons Birddog.* New York: Howell Book House, 1995.

Tarrant, Bill. *Training the Hunting Retriever.* New York: Howell Book House, 1991.

Volhard, Jack and Wendy. *The Canine Good Citizen.* New York: Howell Book House, 1994.

General Titles

Haggerty, Captain Arthur J. *How to Get Your Pet Into Show Business.* New York: Howell Book House, 1994.

McLennan, Bardi. *Dogs and Kids, Parenting Tips.* New York: Howell Book House, 1993.

Moran, Patti J. *Pet Sitting for Profit, A Complete Manual for Professional Success.* New York: Howell Book House, 1992.

Scalisi, Danny and Libby Moses. *When Rover Just Won't Do, Over 2,000 Suggestions for Naming Your Dog.* New York: Howell Book House, 1993.

Sife, Wallace, PhD. *The Loss of a Pet.* New York: Howell Book House, 1993.

Wrede, Barbara J. *Civilizing Your Puppy.* Hauppauge, N.Y.: Barron's Educational Series, 1992.

Magazines

The AKC GAZETTE, The Official Journal for the Sport of Purebred Dogs. American Kennel Club, 51 Madison Ave., New York, NY.

Bloodlines Journal. United Kennel Club, 100 E. Kilgore Rd., Kalamazoo, MI.

Dog Fancy. Fancy Publications, 3 Burroughs, Irvine, CA 92718

Dog World. Maclean Hunter Publishing Corp., 29 N. Wacker Dr., Chicago, IL 60606.

Videos

"SIRIUS Puppy Training," by Ian Dunbar, PhD, MRCVS. James & Kenneth Publishers, 2140 Shattuck Ave. #2406, Berkeley, CA 94704. Order from the publisher.

"Training the Companion Dog," from Dr. Dunbar's British TV Series, James & Kenneth Publishers. (See address above).

The American Kennel Club produces videos on every breed of dog, as well as on hunting tests, field trials and other areas of interest to purebred dog owners. For more information, write to AKC/Video Fulfillment, 5580 Centerview Dr., Suite 200, Raleigh, NC 27606.

chapter 13

Resources

Breed Clubs

Every breed recognized by the American Kennel Club has a national (parent) club. National clubs are a great source of information on your breed. You can get the name of the secretary of the club by contacting:

The American Kennel Club
51 Madison Avenue
New York, NY 10010
(212) 696-8200

There are also numerous all-breed, individual breed, obedience, hunting and other special-interest dog clubs across the country. The American Kennel Club can provide you with a geographical list of clubs to find ones in your area. Contact them at the above address.

Registry Organizations

Registry organizations register purebred dogs. The American Kennel Club is the oldest and largest in this country, and currently recognizes over 130 breeds. The United Kennel Club registers some breeds the AKC doesn't (including the American Pit Bull Terrier and the Miniature Fox Terrier) as well as many of the same breeds. The others included here are for your reference; the AKC can provide you with a list of foreign registries.

American Kennel Club
51 Madison Avenue
New York, NY 10010

United Kennel Club (UKC)
100 E. Kilgore Road
Kalamazoo, MI 49001-5598

American Dog Breeders Assn.
P.O. Box 1771
Salt Lake City, UT 84110
(Registers American Pit Bull Terriers)

Canadian Kennel Club
89 Skyway Avenue
Etobicoke, Ontario
Canada M9W 6R4

National Stock Dog Registry
P.O. Box 402
Butler, IN 46721
(Registers working stock dogs)

Orthopedic Foundation for Animals (OFA)
2300 E. Nifong Blvd.
Columbia, MO 65201-3856
(Hip registry)

Activity Clubs

Write to these organizations for information on the
activities they sponsor.

American Kennel Club
51 Madison Avenue
New York, NY 10010
(Conformation Shows, Obedience Trials, Field
Trials and Hunting Tests, Agility, Canine Good

Citizen, Lure Coursing, Herding, Tracking,
Earthdog Tests, Coonhunting.)

United Kennel Club
100 E. Kilgore Road
Kalamazoo, MI 49001-5598
(Conformation Shows, Obedience Trials, Agility,
Hunting for Various Breeds, Terrier Trials and
more.)

North American Flyball Assn.
1342 Jeff St.
Ypsilanti, MI 48198

International Sled Dog Racing Assn.
P.O. Box 446
Norman, ID 83848-0446

North American Working Dog Assn., Inc.
Southeast Kreisgruppe
P.O. Box 833
Brunswick, GA 31521

Trainers

Association of Pet Dog Trainers
P.O. Box 3734
Salinas, CA 93912
(408) 663–9257

American Dog Trainers' Network
161 West 4th St.
New York, NY 10014
(212) 727–7257

**National Association of Dog Obedience
Instructors**
2286 East Steel Rd.
St. Johns, MI 48879

Associations

American Dog Owners Assn.
1654 Columbia Tpk.
Castleton, NY 12033
(Combats anti-dog legislation)

Delta Society
P.O. Box 1080
Renton, WA 98057-1080
(Promotes the human/animal bond through
pet-assisted therapy and other programs)

Dog Writers Assn. of America (DWAA)
Sally Cooper, Secy.
222 Woodchuck Ln.
Harwinton, CT 06791

National Assn. for Search and Rescue (NASAR)
P.O. Box 3709
Fairfax, VA 22038

Therapy Dogs International
6 Hilltop Road
Mendham, NJ 07945